The Alternative Wedding Book

Create a beautiful wedding that reflects your values & doesn't cost the earth

NORTHSTONE

Cover design: Lois Huey Heck
Cover photo: James Taylor
Japanese lantern artwork: Margaret Kyle
Consulting art director: Robert MacDonald

Permissions:

Two prayers from *Flames of the Spirit* by Ruth C. Duck, copyright 1985. Reprinted with the permission of the Pilgrim Press.

Northstone Publishing acknowledges the financial support of the Government of Canada, through the Book Publishing Industry Development Program, for its publishing activities.

Northstone Publishing is an imprint of Wood Lake Books Inc., an employee owned company, committed to caring for the environment and all creation. Northstone recycles, reuses and composts, and encourages readers to do the same. Resources are printed on recycled paper and more environmentally friendly groundwork papers (newsprint), whenever possible. The trees used are replaced through donations to the Trees for Canada Program sponsored by Scouts Canada. Ten percent of all profit is donated to charitable organizations.

Canadian Cataloguing in Publication Data
Main entry under title:

The alternative wedding book

Includes bibliographical references.
ISBN 1–55145–081–x

1. Weddings--Planning. 2. Marriage service. 3. Wedding etiquette
BJ2051.A77 1996   395'.22   C95–91129–8

Published by
Northstone Publishing
an imprint of Wood Lake Books Inc.
Kelowna, BC, Canada
1.250.766.2778
info@woodlake.com
www.joinhands.com

Printing 9 8 7 6 5 4

Printed in Canada
Friesen Printers

Contents

Introduction

A Guide to Planning
Out-of-the-Ordinary Celebrations

When two people decide to wed, they hear over and over again, however subtly, that the "perfect" wedding must include: first, a 2-carat diamond engagement ring... then, a white satin wedding gown with intricate lace and pearl beads... tailored tuxedos with matching cummerbunds... beautiful flower arrangements spray-painted to match the wedding color scheme... gold-embossed invitations... elaborate reception hall and live band... gourmet food and pastries... a three-tiered wedding cake with a water fountain and plastic reproduction of the couple...

Unfortunately, these commercially prescribed aspects often overshadow the meaning of the event for these two people, their families, and friends. So much time, energy, and money is spent on producing the "perfect" wedding that the focus becomes blurred. The wedding becomes a "social event" rather than a significant religious or personal celebration.

This book offers engaged couples, clergy, and other people alternatives to the bridal magazines and professional wedding consultants. It is very difficult to get beyond consumer pressures and childhood images. After all, our wedding day is one of the most important events in our lives. We labor to symbolize our "unequaled" love with an unequaled celebration. Too often, though, we don't know how to go about planning a truly fulfilling celebration.

This book will encourage you to use your imagination as you incorporate your values and family and ethnic traditions in planning meaningful wedding celebrations. It offers practical advice and personal stories from people who wanted more than the *status quo* wedding and chose to have alternative celebrations instead. It also offers ideas for second marriage ceremonies and vow renewals.

PART 1, "Outward Signs of Inner Values: What Matters for Your Wedding?" gives a firm foundation and support as you begin thinking of wedding alternatives.

PART 2, "Create Your Own Ceremony: Beyond 'Here Comes the Bride,'" will guide you as you try to incorporate your own values and words to create a wedding that is yours alone. This book will be especially helpful when used in discussions with your officiant.

PART 3, "Planning an Alternative Wedding: Food, Flowers, and Festivities," offers alternative ideas for invitations, flowers, clothing, photography, food, and other aspects of the wedding.

To offer you guidelines for scheduling your wedding celebrations, it also includes a "Wedding Timeline/Checklist."

Finally, the "Budget Worksheet" will help you plan expenses and keep track of them along the way.

Outward Signs of Inner Values

What Matters for Your Wedding?

by Mark and Eileen Summit

Matt and Michelle stood smiling at each other beneath the huppah *carried by Matt's siblings. It was made of over 60 unique muslin squares, hand-decorated by family and friends. During the Christian/Jewish wedding, held in an outdoor arboretum, her father offered traditional Jewish blessings to the couple, and his parents read traditional Christian prayers. The rest of the ceremony was a beautiful combination of these two ancient religions, and included elements of Native American tradition and a respect for the earth.*

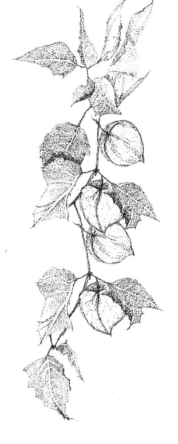

❁

Pat and Mary had been married years earlier in a quiet outdoor setting near a river, in the presence of their friend, a Christian minister, and two witnesses. No other friends and family were present. The beauty of the scenery and the quiet nature of their ritual reflected values of simplicity and conscious use of resources. Over eight years later, strongly involved in a campus ministry Catholic community, and with their first child on its way, they again publicly acknowledged their commitment to their marriage through a nuptial blessing ritual that took place during the Mass.

❁

Chris and Suzy were married in their neighborhood church. They involved their weekly prayer group in their

*marriage preparation process, including an engagement
ceremony during which they exchanged beaded necklaces,
which their friends prayed over. A week before the wedding, the group again gathered to talk about the meaning of weddings and the value of marriage. After the
two recently married couples in the group renewed their
vows, the wedding rings belonging to Chris and Suzy
were passed around so that each person could offer blessings for the couple and their union. On the day of the
wedding, friends gathered just after dawn to begin the
day with communal prayer and singing. Together the
group baked the Eucharistic bread, which would be used
in the ceremony that afternoon.*

❀

How many of us have dreamed, since we were very
young, of getting married? We would walk down
the aisle in our gorgeous white gown, a veil and a
train flowing behind. Or we would be dashingly
handsome in our tuxedo, waiting to marry a most
exquisitely beautiful bride. With admiring friends
and smiling family present, our beloved would look
us in the eye, and say, for all the world to hear, "I
do!" And then we would live happily ever after.

Childhood dreams of weddings tend to focus exclusively on the external things – the gown or tuxedo, the flowers, the rings, etc. – often ignoring
the deeper reality of weddings. Many couples,
sparked by these dreams and fueled by the pressures of family and society, fail to move beyond the
outward traditional symbols in order to seek the
deeper, richer meaning of the event for their lives.
In doing so, they miss an opportunity to make the
wedding truly their own.

The couples mentioned above made a different
choice, one rooted in personal values and mean-

ingful symbols and traditions. They developed intentional wedding rituals which reflected the love that had grown between them, and the new sense of family which was given public recognition during their weddings.

They integrated their histories and their values into their celebrations, and incorporated traditions that had genuine meaning for them. By doing so, their weddings were more fulfilling for them than the typical wedding. Rather than providing a lavish spectacle adorned with hollow, meaningless trappings, they celebrated what mattered most to them: their union, their new family, their love for each other, and their love for their community and the world.

Too often our culture sees the wedding as separate from marriage, a one-time event that is disconnected from the life together that follows. We believe a couple must begin to see their wedding as part of the process of becoming married to make their wedding truly meaningful. A ceremony which incorporates the values of the couple can then become a firm stepping stone to a marriage relationship of commitment and stability.

Unfortunately, it is not easy for a couple to make conscious, meaningful choices for their wedding celebration. All too often their creativity and imagination are stifled by numerous social, familial, and religious expectations, many of which have evolved over hundreds of years. The pressures on a couple to perform in a traditionally acceptable, status quo manner can be enormous. Due to this reality it is helpful to briefly examine some of the history of marriage and weddings, thereby better understanding the influence of tradition on contemporary ceremonies and celebrations.

Historical background

To marry, join, or mate is an age-old tradition. And yet the manner of ritualizing the coming together of two lives has been quite varied across religions, cultures, and eras of our human history.

While comprehensive study of the history of marriage is beyond the scope of this piece, Mark Ishee (*Wedding Toasts and Traditions: Sample Toasts and the Origins of Customs*, Brentwood, Tenn.: J.M. Productions, 1986), provides a useful framework. Ishee writes,

> *Marriage as we know it is very different from marriage in former times. Until the Middle Ages, a king could marry his first cousin, a priest [would often] have a wife and several concubines... Marriage has often been used as a tool to gain political power, and until comparatively recently a woman often had no voice in choosing her husband.*

The author points to three stages in the history of marriage: Marriage by force; marriage by contract, and marriage by mutual love.

Marriage by force is indicated in our earliest historical record. A man captured a woman, generally from another tribe (often because of incest taboos). This testified to his strength in warfare. The earliest "best man" aided a friend in the capture of a bride.

According to Ishee, the honeymoon is a relic of the days of marriage by capture as well. Frequently the tribe from which a warrior stole a bride came looking for her, and it was necessary for the warrior and his new wife to go into hiding to avoid being discovered. The honeymoon evolved as symbolic of the period of time during which the bride and groom hid until the bride's kin grew tired of looking for her.

It is clear why marriage by contract developed in time: the revenge exacted by one tribe on another for taking one of their women was costly. At some point, compensation began to be delivered for the stolen woman in an effort to avoid vengeance. Preventing tribal warfare and compensating furious family members led to a property exchange: livestock, land, or another woman would be exchanged for the bride. As Ishee points out:

> The very word "wedding" betrays the great stage of wife purchase through which marriages passed. The "wed" was the money, horses, or cattle which the groom gave as security and as a pledge to prove his purchase of the bride from her father. From this wed we derive the idea of "wedding" or "pledging" the bride to the man who pays the required security for her.

As time went on, this "bride's price" took the form of elaborate presents given by the groom to the bride's parents. Negotiated over long periods of time, the sending and receiving constituted that the marriage contract was sealed. This tradition can still be found in many countries throughout the world.

In some cultures, land, livestock, and other valuables were given to the groom in the form of a dowry. These goods were offered as compensation to the groom when he assumed the burden of supporting a woman.

Such practices of marriage by contract lasted in England until the middle of the 16th century. The modern practice of "giving the bride away" has its

roots in the belief that the bride was property given
by the father to the groom. In fact, the phrase "to
have and to hold" comes from Old English property transactions.

Marriage by mutual love was rare until fairly recently. You did not marry for love; rather, you were
expected to love the one you married. Ishee states:

*It was not until the 9th or 10th century that
women gained the privilege of choosing or re-
fusing their husbands according to their own
judgment. Rare exceptions to this are recorded
since primitive times, where women claimed the
right to select their mates...*

The practice of elopement was an early aspect of
marriage by mutual love. It allowed a woman to
marry a man of her choosing, rather than one who
met her parents' specifications.

Wedding and Marriage Today
The above are but a few examples of the roots of
the modern marriage ceremony. We live, however,
in a completely different world than did our an-
cestors of previous centuries. More recent historical factors have combined to give us cause to re-
examine traditions and history in a new light.

The change in the status of women is one factor
that significantly affected the way our culture views
weddings and marriage. Throughout the 20th century, social attitudes in North America have been
shifting. Women now expect and demand a more
equal status with men; we have indeed moved a
long way from the days of capture and coercion of
females into marriage.

Over the past few decades an increased number of
people – for political, economic, or sexual reasons

– have chosen lifestyles that do not include marriage. Even though marriage has become more of an option of life than a necessity of life, many people choose to express their commitment and partnership within the institution of marriage.

Weddings still abound, and the media have recently proclaimed a new era of romance. "The Wedding" has taken on almost mythic status, supported by a burgeoning "wedding industry" that boasts millions of dollars in sales annually. Newspapers, magazines, and tabloids chronicle the weddings of superstars in the entertainment world, or of royalty... Who can forget the hoopla surrounding the wedding of England's Prince Charles and Lady Diana?

The happiness promised by the media cannot sustain itself. Having not found a "Mr. or Ms. Right" who will save the day and make everything perfect, some give up rather than undertake the serious work of marriage. They separate, divorce, or have extramarital affairs in the hope of finding that elusive ideal. Eventually the excitement of the new relationship leads to talk of commitment, and then plans for another wedding are made, and the cycle of disillusionment begins again.

While modern wedding ceremonies retain religious and secular symbolism and tradition, presenting colorful and romantic scenarios, they often lack the substance that truly expresses the marriage commitment. Couples wishing for more meaningful and personal ceremonies should ask themselves, "Does this symbol have meaning to me today? Does this tradition reflect our values enough to be highlighted on this important day? Are we succumbing to consumer pressures to include some unnecessary elements?"

Choosing an Alternative

In spite of various pressures, expectations, and prescribed rituals, you have the power to create a very meaningful, personal wedding ritual. Rather than being passively led by prefabricated timelines, bridal books and wedding lists, you can have the courage to move beyond the external trappings most often associated with weddings. You can create beautiful, highly symbolic, and alternative weddings which will set the tone for the entire life of your marriage.

During the early stages of your relationship as your individual life paths began to merge, you probably noticed your values and lifestyle choices became more and more integrated. The wedding day is an opportunity to symbolically join your lives and proclaim to the world those values which brought you together and which will sustain your married life.

❀

The marriage of Barbara and John was presided over by two ministers, one male and one female. In the Quaker tradition, which was part of Barbara's history, the wedding was simple, with a few readings and long periods of silence. Punctuating the silence were reflections offered by several family and friends for and about the couple.

❀

To be "alternative" with your own wedding can be difficult, but may also offer a great sense of pride and accomplishment. It can be a means of publicly announcing and confirming your lifestyle values.

For example, if a desire to simply display wealth is not a part of your value system, think about what you do believe in. During your preparation process, ask yourselves the following questions:

- What will enhance our ritual giving ourselves to each other?
- What religious or spiritual symbolism conveys our belief about marriage and our joining together as a couple?
- What will bring joy and love to this time we share with our community of support?
- How can we best and most fully celebrate this spirit-filled decision which we today announce?
- What are those things that are especially important to us as a couple that we want to share with the world.
- What beliefs, ideas, or philosophy do we share in common?
- What do we want to remember most from our wedding? Is it important that we have a solemn, prayerful experience, or would we rather have a joyous, upbeat affair.
- Is music a big part of who we are as a couple? What form might that music take?
- Are there friends, support groups, or faith communities whom we want to include in the wedding celebration?
- What traditions are part of our family histories? What traditions other than our own have become important to us?

❁

Nigel and Jan were married outdoors, in the Portland International Rose Garden. Jan arrived with her parents, wearing a beautiful, simple dress borrowed from a friend, and Nigel was escorted by their two female witnesses, one of whom carried their rings in a seashell. The setting reflected their common connection with nature, and the quiet beauty of the ceremony spoke clearly of their shared value of simplicity.

An alternative wedding can, and often does, include various traditional aspects. You may wish to incorporate in the ceremony some prayers, songs, or readings that are familiar to your loved ones, or that have been passed down through your families. These can increase the comfort level of those present so that they can participate more fully in the celebration. Friends and family who are thus helped to feel more at ease may then be more receptive to parts of the ritual that are different or uncommon, those parts that reflect your personal and unique relationship as a couple.

❀

Mary and Bill grew up in the Roman Catholic tradition, but elected to have an outdoor, non-Catholic wedding because of their strong belief in inclusiveness. Their ceremony closely resembled the Catholic Mass, with readings and shared bread, a format that was familiar to family and friends. However, they chose both male and female co-celebrants, a Catholic nun and a Presbyterian minister. They also included a story told dramatically by a storyteller friend. In acknowledgment of Mary's Catholic Italian heritage, she and Bill included some traditional customs at the reception, which made for a rousing time!

❀

We chose to honor both our traditional Catholic backgrounds and our growing alternative value base by planning two wedding celebrations. The first was held in the Catholic church we attended while at college in California, and near where much of our family live; the second happened in the midst of a weekend-long celebration at a retreat house outside Portland, Oregon, our current home.

It was more work than we expected, but having two celebrations meant we could satisfy numerous dreams. The first celebration included our families and followed the Catholic tradition, which we adapted based on our own alternative values. The second followed no pre-existing format, and allowed us to include Native American, creation-centered, and other personally meaningful rituals and symbolism. The two geographic locations enabled more family and old friends to come to the first wedding, while a larger number of our local support community could celebrate with us during the second.

How traditional or non-traditional our wedding celebrations were is not important. Rather, the intentionality and purposefulness which we as a couple brought to our wedding celebrations made them unique or alternative. We can then take that intentionality to the remainder of our marriage journey.

People Centeredness
One of the most important values we as a couple chose to affirm in our wedding rituals was our value for relationships. We were celebrating our belief in "people-centeredness" rather than having the material, thing-centered focus that is so common. This was best illustrated in the composition of the "wedding party" at our California ritual, which consisted of far more people than is typical.

The opening procession was led by six flag-bearers waving beautiful, brightly-colored banners; two of them joined us later in the ceremony for a liturgical dance, one led the congregation in a "movement prayer," and another was one of our official witnesses. They were followed by the two principal readers, and four friends who were involved in preparing the table for communion. Then came a married couple who read petitions, a close friend who was the other witness, and the pianist. This long train of supportive friends was completed by the presiding priest and a female homilist (a conscious choice of ours which is uncommon for Catholic weddings).

Rather than having Eileen "given away" by her father, we adapted the tradition to include our immediate families. While a contemporary song that is special to us was being played, Mark's three brothers proceeded down the aisle, followed by Mark arm-in-arm with his two parents. Likewise, Eileen's brothers and their families preceded her and her parents. When we reached the altar, we each joined our family of origin for a common hug, then went to stand by each other. In this way, we symbolically acknowledged the family from which we came, and the new family we were beginning.

Many other friends and family were also involved. Relatives helped by baking bread and contributing the cups and plates used for communion. The altar cloth was the top side of a quilt, sewn together by members of our faith community; the quilt consisted of 30 individually-designed and crafted squares, made by family and friends (some of whom could not attend the wedding in person). Musically talented friends helped us prepare long before the wedding day, as did the two liturgical dancers. Mark's brother designed and printed the invitation, and helped create the wedding program.

The Oregon celebration gave us an opportunity to include even more people in a conscious way. members of our faith community were the lay celebrants at the ritual, and numerous friends contributed readings and prayers. In addition, a group of six musicians led the group in singing and chanting.

Our wedding rituals were truly joyous and supportive celebrations, and the primary reason was the
involvement of so many important, valued people
in our lives. Each ritual ended in a blessing of us
by our guests; we felt especially thankful, and we
knew that those present would both support us and
help keep us accountable to the commitment we
were making.

Another way we incorporated our people-centered
values into our wedding celebrations was by suggesting that our family and friends consider making a donation in our names to non-profit organizations which we support. In our wedding invitation, we inserted a brief notice that mentioned an
organization working to end world hunger and
another supporting the people of Nicaragua and
gave their addresses. In doing this, we publicly af-
firmed our desire for peace and justice in the world,
and our connection to the global community.

Confronting Consumerism
In addition to wedding gifts, there are many other
expenses associated with weddings. Because weddings are rightly a celebration of abundant joy, it is
inevitable that most weddings, especially if they
include a large number of family and friends, involve spending a large amount of money.

While we do not want to discourage the spirit of
celebration, couples can make choices regarding
the expenses they and their families incur. In this
world of great divisions between materially poor
and the materially wealthy, we encourage you to
avoid the temptation to become over-indulgent
or irresponsibly extravagant.

Many modern trappings may have no particular
significance to a couple. Can they be downplayed

or let go? ask yourself if *things* are taking prec-
edence over *people*, either in your attitude, in the
time given to planning, or in events of the day.

❀

*Michael and Donna were particularly attuned to the
reality of world poverty, and wanted their wedding to
reflect their sensitivity to those who had so little. As a
result, they enlisted the support of their local friends to
organize a potluck wedding reception, choosing not to
spend a fortune on catering. They also suggested in the
wedding invitation that people donate to their Nicaragua sister parish in their names as an alternative to
traditional gift-giving. Friends and family donated over
$2,000.*

❀

Personalizing the Ritual
While our entire wedding ritual demonstrated our
love for each other and our desire to share our life
together, our vows offered a special opportunity to
witness our love. We rewrote the traditional vows
to reflect our own history and values. We each made
a unique personal statement to each other, and
completed the vows with a common statement of
commitment.

We further personalized our rituals by rewriting
the traditional prayers to use inclusive, non-sexist
language, wording it to reflect our belief that people should not be referred to as "men" and God as
exclusively male. Many churches now offer inclusive language liturgies and music.

Because we had met in a college class on liturgical
dance, and had later been involved in a company
of liturgical artists, we closed our ceremony with a

sacred dance with two friends. We wanted to share with those whom we love our belief that our marriage is a lifelong dance with each other, moving ever closer to the Creator.

Many couples decide to use traditional language and rituals in their wedding ceremony. For many, this may be highly important and meaningful. After spending a great deal of time struggling to personalize their ceremony, one couple realized that the traditional wording, symbols and music really reflected their feelings. For others, going along with cultural, family, and/or church expectations constitutes a lack of choosing. We encourage you to consciously work to make your wedding your own, so it reflects who you are as a couple in the world.

The Wedding is a Foundation
A wedding ritually celebrates the union of two people and their families. Therefore, it often highlights issues or conflicts that may be present with either person's family of origin. Whether or not either partner has been married before, or have lived together before marriage, the ritual involves separation—leaving one family and beginning another. Making choices together during the planning of the wedding helps solidify the partnership and eases the transition from the past to the future.

Our wedding celebrations helped cement a secure foundation for our future together. Our actions, our dress, the environment, and the arrangement of all aspects of the celebrations made a statement of who we are as a couple, what we want our shared life to be about, and how we view our friends, family, and the world.

Perhaps the most alternative aspect of our marriage was the choosing and proclaiming of the new family name we were taking: Summit. During our preparation for marriage, we discussed at length our dilemma about choosing a name. With our strong Christian feminist values, we valued both the commonality of a single shared family name and the desire not to participate in the patriarchal tradition of a woman taking the man's name. Taking Eileen's family name would have been too reactive, and hyphenating the names felt overly formal and stiff.

Thus, creating a new name was the only option that "fit" us. After making the decision, we opened ourselves to being inspired by the Spirit, and the name "Summit" came to us, a name that has spiritual, natural, and political significance. The homilist in our Catholic ceremony reinforced our choice, making reference to the many times in the Bible that God gave individuals a new name. We, like them, were following the Spirit in beginning a new phase in our journey.

We have been married for nearly three years now, and the memories of our wedding are still fresh and life-giving. Choosing, and then celebrating, an alternative wedding, one that reflected and celebrated our unique partnership, was a highlight in our lives. The unity that was developed during the process of planning, celebrating, and remembering our weddings continues to sustain us through the sometimes mundane and stressful pace of daily living. We are now able to go further in sharing our deepest selves with each other.

We wish you much joy, and hope that your wedding celebration is a meaningful and treasured experience. May it be but one of many wonderful steps of a long road you walk together.

Eileen and Mark Summit grew up as Eileen Bradley and Mark Honeywell, in San Jose, California, and Houston, Texas, respectively. They met at the University of Santa Clara, and held the first of their two wedding rituals in the campus' Mission Church. Both have worked as full-time volunteers in non-profit organizations and both served as staff members for the Jesuit Volunteer Corps, Northwest. They have lived in community with others for the past several years, and currently share a home with another couple. Eileen and Mark are currently working as social workers in Portland, Oregon, and Vancouver, Washington, and have come to love the beauty of the great northwest.

Resources

Arisian, Khoren. *The New Wedding: Create Your Own Marriage Ceremony*. New York: Random House (Vintage Books), 1973.

The Beacon Group, eds. *Perspectives on Marriage*. Chicago: ACTA Publications, 1988.

Blood-Patterson, Peter, *Rise Up Singing*. Bethlehem, PA: Sing Out Corporation, 1988.

Brill, Mordecai (Jewish), Marelene Halpin (Catholic) and William Genne (Protestant), eds. *Write Your Own Wedding*. New York: Association Press, 1973.

Burtness, Eric and Paula. *The Wedding Handbook*. Minneapolis: Augsburg Fortress, 1989.

Champlin, Joseph M. *Together For Life*. Notre Dame: Ave Maria Press, 1975.

Emrich, Duncan. *The Folklore of Weddings and Marriages*. New York: American Heritage Press, 1970.

Hathorn, Raban, William Genne and Mordecai Brill, eds. *Marriage: An Interfaith Guide for All Couples.* New York: Association Press, 1970.

Hodsdon, Nick. *The Joyful Wedding: New Songs and Ideas for Celebrations.* Nashville: Abingdon, 1973.

Homburg, Arthur, ed. *A New Wedding Service for You: Nineteen Orders of Worship for the Prospective Bride and Groom.* Lima, OH: C.S.S. Publishing Co., Inc., 1985.

Ishee, Mark. *Wedding Toasts and Traditions: Sample Toasts and the Origins of Customs.* Brentwood, TN: J.M. Productions, 1986.

Knight, George W. *Wedding Ceremony Idea Book: How to Plan a Unique and Memorable Wedding Ceremony.* Brentwood: J.M. Publications, 1984.

Knight, George W. *The Second Marriage Guidebook: Dealing with the Unique Factors of the Second Wedding.* Brentwood, TN: J.M. Productions, 1984.

Luther, Donald J., ed. *Preparing for Marriage: A Guide for Christian Couples.* Minneapolis: Augsburg Fortress Publishers, 1992.

Munro, Eleanor, ed. *Wedding Readings.* New York: Viking Penguin Books, 1989.

Parrigin, Perry and Van Shaw. *Selecting Organ Music for Weddings* (cassette tape). (Write to Parrigin and Shaw, Presbyerian Student Center, 100 Hitt St., Columbia, MO 65201.)

Seligson, Marcia. *The Eternal Bliss Machine: America's Way of Wedding.* New York: William Morrow and Co., Inc., 1973.

Snow, M. Lawrence. *Your Ministry of Planning a Christian Wedding.* Nashville: Discipleship Resources, 1988.

Somerville Wall, Wendy. *The Creative Wedding Handbook*. New York: Paulist Press, 1973.

Thomas, John L., S.J. *Beginning Your Marriage*. Chicago: ACTA Publications, 1987.

Urbine, William F. *To Trust Again: A Remarriage Preparation Program*. Chicago: ACTA Publications, 1990.

Denominational Worship Books
Check with your local clergy person.

Create Your Own Ceremony

Beyond "Here Comes the Bride"

Heidi K. Roy

When my husband and I decided to marry almost three years ago, we knew we wanted an alternative wedding. An elaborate and expensive wedding was not only out of our budget, but was in conflict with our values and wants. A friend recently reminded me of my words at the time: "It is more important to us to be married than to get married."

The belief that had the most impact on our wedding plans was that our marriage, our union, was very personal and sacred. Therefore, we told few people; only the officiant and two witnesses knew beforehand. While there are many very good reasons for including family and friends during this special time, our decision allowed us to focus on each other and the important step we were taking. And our plans were free of others' expectations and demands.

We were married on the third green of the golf course my husband spends countless hours nurturing and maintaining. We were married by my colleague at the time, a United Methodist minister. This combination signified for us a coming together of our different interests and unique talents. Our attire was simple – clothes which had been in our closets and adorned our bodies more than once before; guests were few – the two witnesses and a video camera person in all.

Our wedding ceremony was "ecumenical," in that it was co-officiated by an Episcopal priest and a Disciples of Christ minister, both old friends. One of our grandmothers helped us choose the hymns from among her old favorites. One of the ministers opened the service by recounting the story of our reunion, entitled "Connections," reflecting on the way many friends around the world had participated in this journey.

We entered the church arm in arm followed by a procession or our closest family members. This symbolized, according to Vietnamese custom, the accompaniment of our families with us in this important passage and life event.

An especially meaningful part of the service was when three close friends who have known us since the beginning of our courtship each stood up in the congregation to offer words of encouragement and blessing. Their meditations reflected their hopes for

The celebration afterward was different, however. After explaining to shocked parents in Detroit Metropolitan Airport that we married earlier that day, we spent ten days "honeymooning" with family and friends. Those ten days were a true wedding celebration, and were filled with special moments I will never forget.

While it took little thought or discussion to decide what kind of wedding we wanted, one thing I regret giving little thought to is the wording and content of the actual ceremony. I remember thinking it was important to me to have something traditional in such a non-traditional wedding. However, after reading the many ideas people shared as we developed these wedding materials, I couldn't help but wish I had given it more thought. I was deeply moved by the love, commitment, and uniqueness which came through the words written especially by and for the couple being married. Their choice of words, music, prayers, and readings really expressed who they are both together and as individuals. As Arthur Homburg in *A New Wedding Service for You* (C.S.S. Publishing Co., Inc., 1985) explained it, "What the writing or altering of services did for the couple was to allow them to make the service their own. They had to wrestle with the meaning of each part and how it applied to them personally."

Whether you opt for a traditional ceremony or you decide to personalize all or parts of it, make sure you consider the many alternatives available to you. Talk with your partner and make a conscious decision based on your values and wants.

Beginning to Plan

First of all, you will need to decide what kind of marriage ceremony you would like – religious or civil ceremony, traditional, contemporary, etc. Talk with your partner about your preferences and come to an agreement. This is especially important when partners come from different faiths. Take family values, traditions, and expectations into account. Your families might have strong feelings about this issue, so it is a good idea to discuss this with them as well. Remember, though, the final decision should be yours.

our happiness as well as their admonitions that we "learn to love one another's differences" – and that we work hard to see that our marriage not become a self-absorbed affair but a pouring out and an offering of love and service to those in greater need.

Michael and
Thanh-Xuan Knowles
Washington, DC

Imagine the thought that went into one Quaker couple's decision on the kind of marriage ceremony they wanted. In a handout for the ceremony, the couple explained their choice of a "Celebration of Commitment" –

> The Atlanta Friends Meeting welcomes you to this meeting for worship to celebrate the commitment of Ann Bryn Houghton and Vince Brown. Ann Bryn and Vince have chosen not to call their ceremony a marriage because they believe that being joined together in the presence of the Spirit and friends requires a deep commitment that need not be sanctioned by the State...

Choosing an Officiant and Location

The next step is choosing an officiant or officiants. Whether you plan to have a religious or civil ceremony, take some time to carefully consider whom you want to officiate. If you and your partner are from different religious backgrounds, consider the possibility of having an officiant from each faith.

If you choose an officiant(s) whom neither of you knows well, spend time discussing your backgrounds and relationship with her/him. These discussions will help you seek the officiant's assistance in personalizing the ceremony. Many religious officiants require some pre-marital counseling to explore issues the couple may encounter in their marriage. There are many good resources available to help engaged couples explore these issues; see the resource listing at the end of the first chapter, "Outward Signs of Inner Values."

When you decide on an officiant(s), make sure to ask about any restriction right away, especially if you plan to customize your ceremony. And if you plan to marry at a non-religious site, make sure it is acceptable to the officiant. When planning a second marriage ceremony, an officiant might also suggest roles in the ceremony for children from previous marriages if any are involved.

When deciding on number of attendants, guests, and other elements of the ceremony, keep in mind the limitations – size, lighting, weather, etc. – of the location you have chosen. For example, if you chose an outdoor setting, you might not want to perform the lighting of unity candles, especially on windy days. Refer to the section on "Choosing a Location" in "Planning an Alternative Wedding: Food, Flowers and Festivities" for more information.

Interreligious or Intercultural Weddings
When planning an interreligious or intercultural wedding, you may want to blend religious or ethnic customs for a ceremony which expresses who each of you is. Some couples choose to incorporate meaningful customs from a broad range of religions and cultures to make the ceremony more inclusive. If you plan to invite guests from many different backgrounds, you could help make people feel more comfortable by including different

customs. One couple observed their wedding ceremony in both English and Spanish, with each giving their vows in a different one of these languages.

Choosing Elements of the Ceremony

In the United States, the only thing required to constitute a marriage is the signature of a clergyperson, judge, sea captain, or other qualified person on a validated marriage license. In Canada, things are not much different. Minimum requirements vary slightly from province to province, but the signature of a provincially certified person licensed to marry, on a valid marriage certificate, is a common requirement. However, most people in Canada and United States desire a celebration filled with rituals, actions, words, and music. Customs and requirements vary greatly from culture to culture, faith to faith, denomination to denomination, and church to church. Consult your clergyperson or officiant early in the planning process to determine which aspects of the ceremony are necessary and how much freedom you have in changing words and arrangement of the different elements.

Spend time reviewing the following elements with your partner, the officiant, and family and friends, if you wish. What parts of the ceremony are most important to you? Which are not? What parts of the ceremony are important to others close to you? Where are you willing to make compromises? Take notes during your discussions and compile an outline you can revise as your ceremony develops. (Note: Don't limit yourselves to these elements. Feel free to consider others.)

Finally, remember there is no "perfect" recipe. As soon as possible, begin planning your ceremony by talking with each other about your mutual values and

As two volunteer refugee workers in Vietnam with the Mennonite Central Committee, we like to say we fell in love clinging to each other in the darkness of our makeshift bomb shelter during a mortar attack on our town. It's almost true. The wedding in our small town Quang Ngai house was international, interreligious and interesting! A Vietnamese Catholic priest gave the homily. A Vietnamese Protestant pastor married us. Two Buddhist co-workers were bridesmaids.

Earl Martin
Akron, Pennsylvania

priorities. Discuss what kind of lifestyle you will lead together and consider how you can express your values through the ceremony. If possible, observe other weddings for ideas or talk with other couples who were recently married.

Whether you are planning a ceremony where both partners have never been married, one which will be a second marriage for one or both of the partners, or a vow renewal service, we offer many ideas here. Read through the different parts and decide which ones suit you and your situation. Let these ideas inspire you to develop your own unique ceremony.

MUSIC

Having music at weddings dates back to the days when noise was thought to keep evil spirits away. For present-day weddings, appropriate music can add solemnity, praise, and joyous celebration to the wedding ceremony. There are unlimited pieces of music, both traditional and contemporary, to choose from. Talk with your partner about what music has special meaning to you: as you were growing up, as you dated, etc. Also consider music which has cultural or family importance.

Consider involving talented family and friends in the ceremony by asking them to sing a solo or duet. Or ask them to organize a choir. Perhaps they can offer their talent as a wedding gift to you. You might also choose one or more appropriate hymns which can involve the participation of all guests.

There are a number of places to incorporate music into your ceremony. Traditionally, the prelude includes instrumentals played by an organist or pianist as guests are seated. During the processional, the tempo of the music usually picks up

We wanted lots of music. I turned to a long-time friend who lived in San Francisco. A gifted singer and composer, he was sensitive to our needs and plan. He wrote a gorgeous piece for us based on 1 Corinthians 13, located the dancer, and arranged for all the musicians needed to do what was mostly a chamber music type of concert before the service.

Alice Ann Glenn
Monterey, California

During "Song of the Soul" the two of us showered family and guests with confetti as a symbol of our exuberance!

Ann Sensenig and
Daniel Erdman
Lancaster, Pennsylvania

and the wedding party enters. Hymns, vocal music, and contemplative instrumentals can be inserted in various places throughout the ceremony. During one ceremony, a soloist sang "The Lord's Prayer" as the couple knelt in prayer following their vows. As the wedding party leaves during the recessional, you might choose joyous hymns of praise or celebratory instrumentals. One couple, as they turned from the altar for the recessional, asked guests to join them in a rousing rendition of *I've Got That Joy, Joy, Joy, Joy Down in My Heart*. It is best not to have any background music when people are speaking during the ceremony. Music during these times makes it difficult for people to hear, and distracts from the sentiments being shared.

When planning a church wedding, there might be some restrictions on music choices and placement. Check with the officiant or music director on this. The following is a list of some possibilities:

Instrumentals
Aria, When Thou Art Near, by J.S. Bach
"Sinfonia" to *Wedding Cantata No. 196*, by J.S. Bach
Finale from Suite in D, by William Boyce
Fanfare, by Guy Eldridge
Larghetto, by C.F. Handel
"Finale" from *Royal Fireworks*, by C.F. Handel
Vals Criollo, by Antonio Lauro
Trumpet Tune, by Michael McCabe
Vocalise, by Rachmaninoff
Symphony of the Psalms, by Stravinsky
Fantasia on a Theme by Thomas Tallis, by Vaughan Williams

Our wedding was on the one month anniversary of the start of the Persian Gulf War and we sang "Dona Nobis Pacem" (Lord Grant Us Peace) in rounds. It was one of the most transcendant moments of the whole ceremony to hear the voices of families and friends weaving together, and in my mind, spiraling upward and surrounding us all.

Laurel Kearns
Atlanta, Georgia

When planning our vow renewal, I didn't feel that "Here Comes the Bride" would be appropriate so we picked an instrumental version of a song called, Love Can Make You Happy, from 1969. For the solo it was tough to find an appropriate song with a message of continuing love and devotion rather than a new beginning. We went with a contemporary Christian song called *Perfect Union* which speaks of depending on God in good and bad times. The recessional music was a lively piano version of another oldie – *Oh How Happy You Have Made Me.*

Michelle DeLoach Harper
Forest Park, Georgia

The wedding procession of my daughter and son-in-law involved two families... the order of the procession was the cross-bearer (one of Greg's two nephews); Greg between his parents; followed by his sister, her husband (the best man), and their second son; next, came Michelle's two sisters and brother; then came Michelle walking arm-in-arm with her mother and father.

Marilyn A. Cramer
Westminster, Maryland

Hymns

All Creatures of Our God and King

Amazing Grace

Blest Are They

Come, My Way, My Truth, My Life

For the Beauty of the Earth

God of Our Life

Hear Us Now, Our God

In Thee Is Gladness

Joyful, Joyful We Adore Thee

Let all the World In Every Corner Sing

Let's Sing Unto the Lord/Cantemos as Senor

Lord of All Hopefulness

Love Divine, All Loves Excelling

Now Thank We All Our God

O Perfect Love

O Young and Fearless Prophet

The King of Love My Shepherd Is

When Love is Found

Where Charity and Love Prevail

Your Love, O God, Has Called Us Here

Special Vocal Music

The Gift of Love, by Hal Hopson

You Made Us For Each Other, by John Innes

Because You Are God's Chosen Ones, by G. Alan Smith

Bridal Prayer, by Roger Copeland

Wedding Prayer, by Fern Glasgow Dunlap

The Wedding Song, by Paul Stookey

Wedding Blessing, by Wetzler

Wedding Blessing, by Pelz

As You Go On Your Way, by James Engel

Last Night I Had the Strangest Dream I Ever Dreamed, by Bob Dylan

If We Only Have Love, by Jacques Brel

Try to Remember, by the Kingston Trio

Here and Now, by Luther Vandross

Song of the Soul by Chris Williamson

PROCESSIONAL

During the processional, mentioned in the section on music above, the wedding party enters the place the ceremony will occur. If you choose to have a processional and a wedding party, there are many possibilities as to number of attendants and the order they enter. As a couple, spend some time discussing if you want attendants, and if so, how many and who they will be. You don't necessarily have to have a large, traditional wedding party with a maid or matron of honor, a best man, brides-maids, flower girl, and ring bearer. There are many alternatives from which to choose. Some couples choose to have their parents or entire families es-cort them. Others choose not to have attendants at all.

Spend some time considering how the wedding party will enter. In the Russian Orthodox tradition, cou-ples process up the aisle together, following the priests. During one ceremony mentioned in *Write Your Own Wedding* (Follett Publishing Co., 1979), the groom, from the pulpit, read the Song Of Songs as the bride all alone walked up the aisle toward him.

In one English tradition, the entire wedding party walks to the church together in a procession (an age-old custom that protected the couple from jealous ex-suitors). For this procession, a flower girl leads the way, sprinkling petals along the road to signify a happy route through life for the bride and groom.

In Finland, laurel leaves symbolizing fertility are laid outside the town hall or church as a bridal path. A symbolic hand-painted duck or live goose and gan-der (all of which mate for life) are carried in a Ko-rean wedding procession as a reminder of fidelity.

The day of our traditional Hindu wedding, Yatin came to my parents' house. I met him at the door and placed a garland of red roses around his neck, then disappeared into the house. the priest handed Yatin a coconut. Yatin placed it on the ground, stepped on it and broke it. My mother then came and placed a red dot on his forehead using the ring finger of her right hand and welcomed him into the house. Yatin went with the priest and my parents to the small canopy, and the priest began the 2–3 hour ceremony. During the ceremony, my mother's brother came to get me and brought me to the canopy. The priest placed a red chord around Yatin and me and, holding right hands, we walked under the small canopy.

Alka Y. Patel
Jonesboro, Georgia

After Mike (officiant) and we welcomed everyone, my mother welcomed Cliff into our family and Cliff's father welcomed me. They wrote their own greetings – my mother's included a prayer and Cliff's father's was a story – each standing on its own terms. Later, my father and Cliff's mother brought us the rings to exchange.

Kathie Klein
Atlanta, Georgia

WORDS OF WELCOME

Traditionally, the minister or officiant welcomes guests and thanks them for their presence. More recently, some couples have decided to greet their guests themselves. You might also ask a family member(s) to do this for you. Other couples prefer to greet their guests in a wedding service bulletin and eliminate this element from the ceremony.

OPENING WORDS AND SERMON

In many weddings, the officiant makes a short statement on the meaning of marriage, particularly as revealed in the Bible. The officiant may also speak of the significance of the ceremony about to take place. It is also appropriate to include a few words about the couple and their history. Some couples choose to give the opening words themselves or ask friends or family members to participate.

If you choose to have an officiant, friends, or family members give the opening words, talk to them about elements you would like covered. One rabbi in Pacific Palisades, California, asks engaged couples to each write a short paragraph about what attracts them to their partner. He then encourages the couple to read this aloud during the ceremony or he incorporates their words into his sermon.

In addition to these opening words, many ministers plan to give a lengthier sermon on marriage later in the ceremony. Talk with the minister about your preferences and discuss content if possible.

PRAYERS

Prayers offer an added sense of solemnity and praise. During a wedding ceremony, people often pray for God's guidance and direction. Prayers usually include words of thanksgiving for this happy occasion as well. It is also appropriate to offer prayers that show concern for the needs of the world, the poor, and the suffering.

Many churches and officiants offer guidance, including books which provide appropriate prayers.

Often, the officiating minister offers prayers. Some couples say prayers themselves or ask a member of the wedding party or a family member to take part in offering prayers. Prayers said by a parent(s) can have special meaning and impact during a wedding ceremony.

For a second marriage, one couple adapted their wedding ceremony to include adoption prayers and liturgy so the woman and her new stepson could say vows as stepmother and stepchild. And in one Jewish wedding custom, memorial prayers are offered for a deceased parent of either the bride or groom.

SCRIPTURE READINGS

Scripture readings that focus on the meaning of marriage are often a part of a religious wedding ceremony. The officiant may read or refer to Scripture during his/her opening words or sermon. And the officiant, couple, family, or friends may read Scripture passages during other parts of the ceremony. Some couples concerned with Scripture passages which use non-inclusive language, seek out alternative translations or slightly alter the passages. Check with your officiant to become aware of any restrictions concerning Scripture alteration or other issues. (Some denominations have inclusive language lectionaries.)

The Roman Catholic Church is one which places some restrictions on readings. A traditional Catholic wedding mass calls for a reading from the Old

Instead of having a preacher give a meditation, we had several friends talk about commitment and what it meant to them. The ceremony ended with an open mike time where family and friends responded with memories, advice, and blessings.

Carolyn Schrock-Shenk
Lancaster, Pennsylvania

Following the exchange of rings, the homilies and the traditional western vows, we ended the service by reading together to the congregation the Prayer of St. Francis, as our own prayer and aspiration for a life lived together in humility, peace, and sacrificial love.

Michael and
Thanh-Xuan Knowles
Washington, DC

Testament, one from the Epistles, and one from the Gospels. A listing of the permitted readings is usually available to you as you make your choices. The following are some passages commonly used during wedding ceremonies:

Genesis 1:26–31	Matthew 19:3–6
Genesis 2:18–24	Mark 10:6–9
Psalm 33	John 2:1–11
Song of Solomon 2:10–13	John 15:9–17
Song of Solomon 8:6–7	John 17:20–26
Isaiah 54:5–8	Romans 8:31b–39
Isaiah 55:1–3a, 10–13	Romans 12:1-2, 9–13
Jeremiah 31:31–34	1 Corinthians 12:31–
Hosea 2:16–20	13:13
Matthew 5:1–10	Ephesians 5:1–2, 21–33
Matthew 5:13–16	Colossians 3:12–17
Matthew 6:25–33	John 4:7–12
Matthew 7:24–29	Revelation 19:1, 5–9a

COMMUNION

Since Communion can remind us of Christ's first miracle during the wedding feast at Cana, it is appropriate for the couple and their guests to celebrate unity in Christ through this sacramental meal at a church wedding. For some weddings, friends or relatives have baked the bread. And some couples have taken the role of serving Communion to their guests. Especially if your wedding is interreligious or guests are from many different faiths, take time to consider how others might feel during this part of the ceremony.

POETRY AND SPECIAL READINGS

By including poetry and special readings which have been meaningful to you, or ones which express your feelings for each other, you can make the ceremony more personal. Some couples choose to read selections to each other while others ask family members or friends to read some aloud.

The gifts of bread (homemade by one of Michel's sisters) and wine (made by Greg's father), and a monetary gift for St. John's House (our parish's residence, which is offered to one family at a time to help them in their efforts to get back on their feet), were brought forth by both sets of parents and presented to their newly married children, who, in turn, presented them to the presider.

Marilyn A. Cramer
Westminster, Maryland

The following is a list of a few possible poems and readings:

Selections from *The Prophet*, by Kahlil Gibran

Of Triscuits, Bremner Wafers and Dailyness, by Ellen Goodman

The Attitude of Love and *A Universal Love*, by Erich Fromm

Poetry by Elizabeth Barrett Browning and Robert Browning

The House at Pooh Corner, by A.A. Milne

The Velveteen Rabbit, by Margery Williams

Letters on Love, by Rainer Maria Rilke

"94," poem by E.E. Cummings (from *95 Poems*)

THE GIVING IN MARRIAGE

In past times, this element of the wedding was a time for the bride's father to formally "transfer property" of the bride to the groom. Because times and attitudes about marriage and women have changed greatly since the time this custom was instituted, many couples have chosen to drop or amend this practice. Possibilities include changing the wording to, "Who presents this woman..."; or having both sets of parents offer their blessings. Some ceremonies allow time for parents (or all immediate family members) to offer brief statements of love, encouragement, and best wishes for the union. Family members might also give a brief history of each family being joined.

GROUP PARTICIPATION

Many contemporary weddings encourage participation of all those in attendance. Guests are included in the celebrations rather than considered passive observers. One mother-of-the-bride shared with us these words offered by her guests: "I felt like we were all part of the ceremony;" "I had a large part to play, not just watching from a distance while something I

Since my mother was our only living parent, she did the history so everyone who came to the ceremony knew "how we got together" and a bit about each of us.

Alice Ann Glenn
Monterey, California

We called together our family and friends to celebrate with us and to be a community of support and encouragement. They shared in spirited four-part singing. Each family shared briefly, "letting go" and welcoming a new member. And everyone signed a congregational response to our vows which now hangs on our wall.

Andre Gingerlich Stoner
Lancaster, Pennsylvania

couldn't quite hear, nor see, was going on;" "There was so much love in that place, and I was part of it." In addition to partaking in the music through special songs and hymns, guests might read a litany like this one shared by David and Carolyn Schrock-Shenk:

We have witnessed evidence of your love and heard expressions of your faith and hope. You have recognized that human existence is not a solitary walk. The development of your relationship is for us another window through which to view the richness of life-sharing.

Our relationships with you have blended growth and change. You have sought strong participation and welcomed rich diversity. The journey will continue beyond this moment.

We offer our love and support, strong strands that bind us as one. Our own strivings for unity are renewed by your statements of commitment.

Go forward; know God; be encouraged. We will remind you of these commitments. We will rediscover strength through your desire to serve others and reach out. We will share wisdom and celebrate living.

A cord of three strands is not easily broken.

For one wedding ceremony, guests were asked to bring bells as symbols of joy. Guests were encouraged to ring the bells at different times throughout the ceremony. One African custom calls for the bride's guests to line up on one side of the room, the groom's guests on the other. They then walk forward to meet in the middle, embrace, and then switch sides. This symbolizes the marriage of two families.

A Quaker wedding includes time for silent meditation, during which guests may offer words of encouragement and love. Another Quaker custom calls for guests to sign a marriage certificate, committing themselves to foster the union. Here is a sample certificate:

Certificate of Commitment

Whereas Ann Bryn Houghton, daughter of Gaynell Gilbert Houghton and Peter Houghton, and Vincent Edward Brown, son of Bernice Putnam Brown and Louis Brown, having declared their intentions of commitment to each other at the Atlanta Monthly Meeting of the Religious Society of Friends held at Atlanta, Georgia, their celebration was allowed by that meeting.

This is to certify that for the accomplishment of their intentions on this 17th day of the eighth month of 1991, they, Ann Bryn Houghton and Vincent Edward Brown, appeared in a meeting for worship held at the Atlanta Meeting. Ann Bryn taking Vince by the hand did on the solemn occasion declare that she with great respect and love, came here in the presence of the Spirit and these friends to take Vince as her loving companion, promising with divine assistance to be a source of strength, comfort, happiness, understanding, joy and love to him as long as they both shall live.

And in that same assembly, Vince did in like manner declare that he took Ann Bryn to be his loving companion, promising with divine assistance to be a source of strength, comfort, happiness, understanding, joy and love to her as long as they both shall live.

And then they, Ann Bryn and Vince in further confirmation thereof, to this certificate set their hands.

And we having been present at the celebration of commitment have as witnesses hereunto set our hands.

Since this was a second marriage for both of us, it was important for our children — who through our wedding were becoming part of a blended family — to feel as much a part of the service as we did. Accompanied by our children, each of us walked to the altar where each child declared his support of the marriage. Family members from both sides and friends also pledged their support and lighted candles as a symbol of their promises.

Janie Howell
Ellenwood, Georgia

During a Thai wedding ceremony the couple sits on the floor in front of the monks, then move to a rail where they sit or kneel. They then place their hands in a horizontal prayer position while elders file past them, pour water on their hands, and offer blessings and words of advice.

If you decide to include participation of guests, you will need to let people know before or during the ceremony what is expected of them. When guests will be asked to read a litany, a prayer, or some other words consider providing the text in a wedding bulletin or special handout.

EXCHANGE OF VOWS

The wording of the vows is the most common element couples choose to personalize. Some choose to make minor changes in the standard vows of a customary ceremony, to make the language more contemporary and/or to substitute words which express greater equality. Others choose to completely rewrite the vows to better express their feelings for each other. Vows might include information as to the couple's backgrounds and need not be the same for both partners. If you choose to write personalized vows, you might begin by writing down feelings you have for your partner, beliefs you have about marriage in general, and thoughts on how you envision your life together. While you may create your vows to each other separately, it is best to share them with each other before the actual ceremony so there are no surprises or uncomfortable feelings. As some religious denominations require key elements be included in the vows, if you plan on a religious ceremony you should check with the officiant before you get too far along.

One Mexican tradition calls for a large loop of rosary beads, symbolizing unity, to be placed in a figure-eight shape around the necks of the couple after they say their vows.

Japanese couples take nine sips of sake, a Japanese wine made from rice, in the *san-san-kudo* ceremony, becoming husband and wife after the first sip. Family members repeat this at the reception.

Depending on whether your ceremony is a first marriage, a second marriage for one or both of you, or a vow renewal ceremony, special considerations might be in order. Michelle DeLoach Harper shared with us this excerpt of her vows for her vow renewal service: "In our years of marriage, times have been better, times have been worse, we have been richer, we

have been poorer, we have been sick, we have been
healthy. I stand here today, ten years and two daugh-
ters later, to tell you, our family and friends, that I
would do it all over again."

While some authors of wedding books suggest keeping vows short – no more than five sentences – some
couples choose to say much longer vows. Dave and
Carolyn Schrock-Shenk created the following vows
for their alternative wedding ceremony:

*I love you, Carolyn. I give you my love as a gift. You
don't need to earn it; you don't need to question it; and
you don't need to fear the loss of it. I commit myself to
loving you for as long as we live.*

*I commit myself to spending a lifetime building a
relationship with you. I commit myself to being as open
to change and growth when we are 50 as when we were
dating. I want us to enjoy our relationship at every step
of the way, even as we seek to grow.*

*I commit myself to continue to grow by absorbing
your strengths. I admire the person you are and have
appreciated your influence in my life. I want to continue
to learn from you about being honest in our relationship, about the willingness to openly express who we are,
and about the value of silence and reflection in our lives.
I want to learn from you about being open to others and
their viewpoints, and about exploring new ideas and
ways of thinking. And I want to learn from you how to
relax, how to have fun, and how to make the everyday
parts of life enjoyable. I also commit myself to working
gently with you on your weaknesses.*

*I commit myself to helping develop your potential
and talents. As your partner, I make my strengths and
energies available to you for the fulfillment of your
dreams. I commit myself to avoid putting role expectations in your way. I want you to be free to develop in
whatever direction is right for you.*

*I commit myself to honesty and openness about my
sense of how God's love and message can be worked out*

*in our lives and with those we meet. I commit myself to
accountability to you and your sense of God's leading.*

*I remember one rainy day when we came so close to
not patching up a difference we had had. But we began
to talk and then to share ideas of what we wanted life to
be. That's when we realized how closely our dreams
matched. I commit myself to resisting the death of our
dreams, to resisting the pressure of compromise and dull-
ness. I commit myself to keeping hope and newness and
growth alive.*

*Carolyn, I love you, and because of that love, I will
listen and talk to you; I will laugh and cry with you; I
will go for walks with you and rub your back. I will live
with you and grow old with you. I will be your partner,
friend, confidant, and lover for a lifetime.*

*I like you, Dave. I enjoy being with you. I trust you. I
believe in you...I love you. The love I commit to you is
permanent and unconditional. You don't have to perform or meet a set of criteria. I simply love you as you
are. Neither of us is perfect, nor is the world we live in
perfect, but I commit myself to loving you even when
things fall short of what we wish for or hope for.*

*I commit myself to keeping our relationship alive
and growing. The pains of growth and change are hard
for me to cope with at times, but the rewards are obvious.
I would not be marrying you today if it hadn't been for
those growth times – times that almost seemed to destroy
us while we were in them. I want to continue that change
process and to find new dimensions for our relationship
as well as individually.*

*I commit myself to continue learning from your
strengths. You have taught me so much about affirma-
tion, about loving myself, and open communication rather
than silent retreat, about sensitivity, about giving. I want
to keep learning from you. I also commit myself to deal
gently with you in your weaknesses.*

*I commit to helping you develop your potential. You
are a person of many talents and abilities. I will support*

*you and encourage you as you find new ways to use and
develop those gifts. I will work hard at freeing you from
role expectations and demands for certain kinds of performance in order to give you the opportunity to do and
be what's right for you.*

*I commit myself to continue searching for new ways
to live out our call to discipleship as followers of Jesus. I
want to discover what that means for us together. I commit myself to being a peacemaker with you – to reach out
to our neighbors both next door and around the world
with the message of love, peace, and justice.*

*And finally, I commit myself to keeping our dreams
alive. We are saying big things here today, and in some
ways we may be idealistic – we have a lot to learn. But I
commit myself to keep on dreaming and to work hard at
keeping those dreams alive.*

*Dave, I love you, and because of that love, I will
both listen and talk to you, laugh and cry with you. I
will go for walks with you and rub your back. I will live
with you and grow old with you. I will be your partner,
friend, confidante, and lover for a lifetime.*

BLESSING AND EXCHANGE OF RINGS/SYMBOLS

If the couple chooses to exchange rings, this is the
time during the ceremony when they place rings on
one another's fingers. Since the exchange of rings
seals or symbolizes the pledges of devotion the couple offer to each other, this element usually comes
right after the exchange of vows. An officiant might
bless the rings with a statement on the symbolism.
This statement can also be said by the couple.

Joseph M. Champlin, in his book *Together For Life*
(Ave Maria Press, 1970), suggests a slight alteration
of the ring exchange. The couple places the ring only
part way on his/her partner's finger, indicating the
giving of oneself to the other. The partner then draws
the ring on the rest of the way him/herself showing
acceptance of that gift and commitment.

While the trend today is toward the double ring ceremony (rather than one in which only the bride is given a ring), alternatives do exist. Take time to consider the importance of this symbol to you. Are there symbols other than rings that you might prefer? (See the section on Rings/Symbols in "Planning an Alternative Wedding: Food, Flowers and Festivities.")

LIGHTING A UNITY CANDLE

This element is becoming more and more common in wedding ceremonies. Usually, two separate candles are lit, one by each set of parents. These two candles represent each partner's separate life. Then near the end of the wedding service, each partner takes one of the candles and lights a single candle. At this time, someone might read an appropriate scripture passage, such as Genesis 2:23–24 which speaks of "two becoming one." The couple might also make some statement about their union.

After the unity candle is lit, sometimes the original candles are extinguished, and other times they are left burning. W. Clyde Tilley, former professor in the Department of Religion and Philosophy at Union University in Jackson, Tennessee, says:

> When all three candles are left burning, this can speak of a mystical participation in which a oneness is formed but in which the constituent personalities are not negated or overridden... [On the other hand], a couple may see a need to emphasize the "forsaking all others" clause in the ceremony and may wish to do it by extinguishing the candles.

Consider the symbolism and make a choice which fits your beliefs.

DECLARATION OF MARRIAGE

This element is a formal statement which declares that the couple is now united. In a church wedding, the officiant often combines this with a charge to the couple to work together at building their relationship and a Christian home. Comments on the holiness and permanence of marriage are often shared as well.

BENEDICTION

This final blessing of the marriage usually takes the form of a short statement and/or prayer given by the officiant, the couple, a friend, or a family member.

RECESSIONAL

Often, the couple leaves the area where the ceremony took place arm-in-arm, followed by their parents and members of the wedding party. Guests might throw rice, confetti, or birdseed as they exit. (Ask church leaders or location management if there are restrictions on throwing rice, etc.) The wedding party members sometimes join to form a receiving line to greet guests as they depart. However, some couples choose to greet guests in a receiving line at the reception.

OTHER

Take some time to think of other elements you might want to include in your ceremony. When Margaret Yackel and Mark Juleen were married in Circle Pines, Minnesota, they created an element which displayed and merged their talents – Mark composed a song and shared it during the ceremony while Margaret did an interpretative dance. Some couples include a peace greeting as an element of their ceremony. The officiant bestows love and peace on the couple with a handshake, invit-

Batak couples of the Philippines sit on the floor facing each other during their wedding ceremony. The ceremony is presided over by an elder and usually two witnesses. With their hands, the couple feeds each other some cooked rice. When this is done, the elder pronounces them married.

During the benediction for a traditional a Jewish wedding, a small, thin glass (wrapped to prevent splintering) is placed on the floor. The groom then breaks the glass as a symbolic recognition of the sorrows of Israel.

In England, newlyweds may pass through an arch of sabers and swords (for servicepeople) pitchforks (for farmers), nightsticks (for police officers) or other appropriate objects.

During our wedding ceremony, the priest joined my hand and Alka's and put rice and nuts (holy foods) in them. We sprinkled the rice and nuts on the shrine as did our parents. Alka's parents washed our feet with a mixture of milk, honey, sugar, ghee and yogurt. (This mixture is a sign of holiness and respect.) The priest then instructed us to circle the shrine seven time while he offered a prayer. Seven is thought to be a lucky number.

Yatin Patel
Jonesboro, Georgia

During a Native American wedding ceremony, the couple drinks from a two-spouted jug to symbolize the joining of two families.

For an Armenian wedding two white doves are released to signify love and happiness.

Crowns of orange blossoms (symbols of purity and loveliness) are placed on both partners' heads during a traditional Greek wedding ceremony. This symbolizes their entrance into the realm of marriage.

ing the couple to exchange a sign with each other – a formal kiss. The peace greeting is then extended to other wedding members and to guests.

Putting It All Together

Now that you have some idea about what elements you would like to include, consider how you might arrange them. Look over the ceremonies that people have shared with us (following the special suggestions for those planning vow renewals or second marriage ceremonies) to get some sense of how the elements can be incorporated into different kinds of ceremonies.

Ideas for Vow Renewal Ceremonies

As one woman wrote to us: "With all the gloomy divorce statistics these days, *staying* married is at least as worthy of a celebration as *getting* married." And that it is!

Renewing your vows and reaffirming your commitment to each other can be a meaningful and important celebration. Couples have many reasons for reaffirming their marriage commitment.

Some repeat their vows shortly after the original ceremony for relatives and friends who live far away and were not able to attend the wedding. Other couples renew their vows to celebrate a milestone anniversary.

One couple found a need to renew their vows following major changes in their lives. Karen Geiger explains:

> *Our life together had taken some unprecedented twists. (Doesn't everyone's?) In the face of those changes, it was important to remind ourselves of*

*the constancy of the feelings we held for each other
and the permanence of the promises we had made
to each other. Five years also seemed to be a good
time to reread our vows, assess our successes and
failures in living up to them, and resolve to make
improvements. Finally, we had found a strong faith
community after our marriage and wanted to restate our commitments to each other before them...*

*When we review our vows at our tenth anniver-
sary next year, I plan to expand on our original
promises to include additional things I now believe
to be important to a good marriage. I have learned
so much about what it means to honor, trust, understand and respect, and how hard those promises
can be to keep. So, I would not delete any of those,
but would add the following: a promise to listen
more and argue less; to compromise; to support and
encourage each other in work and community
endeavors and in our spiritual journeys; to talk
often about our feeling; to make time to have fun
together... The next time around, I would also like
to make promises to my children.*

If you are considering renewing your vows, take
time to talk with your partner about why reaffirming your vows may be important to you. If you decide to plan a vow renewal, discuss the type of ceremony you envision. Use the following list to guide
you in the planning process:

1. A reaffirmation ceremony can be anything from
   a church service to a picnic. You can recreate your
   original wedding, including setting, music, readings, etc. Or you can create an entirely new celebration.

2. The reaffirmation can include just a few people, close friends and immediate family, or a
   larger group. Perhaps, like Karen Heinze Geiger, you may wish to restate your commitments
   before new friends or a new faith community.

3. You can restate your original vows or write new ones. Decide on what is most important to you. Review your original vows. Do they still cover the important promises you feel your marriage is based on? Would others more clearly state your feelings?

4. Include special music and readings, either those used in your original ceremony or others that have taken on special meaning.

5. Some couples wear clothing worn at the original service. Some choose other special outfits or everyday clothing. Would wearing your original wedding attire hold more meaning for you? Or would some other outfit better represent who you are today?

6. While some couples ask the original attendants to be a part of their vow renewal, others ask their children or new friends. Recognizing the importance of family, some couples with children choose to involve their children in some way. It can be quite meaningful to include children in the procession and/or to ask them to offer words of love and encouragement. Still others prefer to have no attendants. Perhaps entering alone arm-in-arm would be more appropriate to your situation.

7. Many couples choose to have a celebration after the vow renewal service. Choices include a pot-luck dinner, a barbecue picnic, a sit-down meal, dinner at a favorite restaurant, etc. Ask yourselves: What kind of post-ceremony gathering do we want, if any? What is in keeping with our budget? Who will be invited?

8. Consider borrowing items you need for the celebration to keep costs at a minimum. When you must squeeze money out of the household

budget to pay for celebration needs, money may be a big concern. Vow renewals don't have to cost a lot of money. Borrow items you need, such as clothing, chairs, eating utensils, table-cloths, candles, etc. (see "Planning an Alternative Wedding: Food, FIowers and Festivities" for more ideas.)

9. If you plan to send out invitations or to have a wedding bulletin, consider including an original wedding photograph or a photo of your family today. This can make the celebration even more personal and can offer guests a memento of the occasion.

Ideas for Second Marriages

More and more weddings celebrate the union of people who are divorced or widowed. While most second-marriage wedding ceremonies are less ex-travagant than first-time weddings, they are just as worthy of a celebration. These weddings bring with them unique situations that couples should consider. The following list suggests some issues to think about:

1. Talk openly and honestly with each other about the shape you see your lives taking. Consider any obstacles you may encounter. Talk frankly about your financial situation. (Will child support pay-ments be taken from the family budget? Will you need to find a larger – and more expensive – house?) Also discuss how you will pay for the wed-ding. This will probably have an effect on the kind of wedding celebration you plan. Recognize you will need to be open to new ways of relating to your partner. Each of you brings different tra-ditions and ways of doing everyday things to the marriage. Be ready to compromise. By working together to plan the wedding, you can begin to find common ground.

2. If one or both of you have children from a previous marriage, consider how this new union will affect them. Be prepared to handle resentments and jealousies. Tell children about your wedding plans right away. Talk to them about their feelings and make them feel an important part of the new family. Consider involving children in the planning process. Take them along to choose a location. Encourage them to make special decorations for the celebration. Ask children to escort you down the aisle. Give children the opportunity to offer words of encouragement during the ceremony. Include a prayer of blessing for your new family. If children are young, make arrangements for someone to keep on eye on them during the wedding.

3. Choose the type of ceremony you would like – church wedding, civil ceremony, simple celebration, traditional wedding, etc. Some second-marriage couples, who want a more relaxed, informal ceremony, plan their wedding at a chapel, at one of their homes, or at a garden or park. Talk about what is important to each of you.

4. Consider creating a wedding ceremony that incorporates your shared values and family traditions. You may want to personalize your vows so they reflect the promises you are making. Use special songs and readings that express your unique situation. (Talk to the officiant about any restrictions on the ceremony content and wording.)

5. Choose and meet with the officiant. Some ministers may not marry people who have been divorced. If you find this is so in your case and

you still want a church ceremony, ask if another officiant can perform the ceremony in your church or find a nearby church that doesn't have this restriction.

6. Many officiants require pre-wedding counseling. A clergyperson can guide you as you explore some of the obstacles you may face. There are also a number of good resources available. (See the list of resources at the end of "Outward Signs of Inner Values.")

7. Discuss your guest list. Do you want a large celebration or an intimate one? Will you invite children? Will you invite ex-relatives who are still close to you? How will this make your partner feel?

8. Second marriages are usually less extravagant. For this reason, couples often choose to have fewer attendants. Some couples choose to have two witnesses. Many couples involve children in the procession. Others enter alone arm-in-arm.

9. Because some etiquette books say a white wedding gown is inappropriate, some women wear ivory or off-white. Others disregard these "rules" and wear white because it is important to them. Second-marriage partners usually choose clothing which is less extravagant. Many couples feel freer to wear simple clothing that they can wear again. Discuss your preferences.

10. Many second-marriage couples have two well-established homes. Therefore, you may wish to discourage guests from giving gifts. It would be appropriate, however, to ask guests to make a donation to a worthwhile cause if they are determined to give a gift.

Sample Ceremonies

SAMPLE ONE

This ceremony, written by Rev. Donna Rose-Heim, a Christian Church (Disciples of Christ) minister in Odessa, Missouri, is best done in a "U" shaped seating arrangement. There is not one minister but many who participate, both lay and ordained.

LITURGICAL CELEBRATION

Prelude
(A variety of family members and friends carry in the elements of worship, i.e. communion elements, candles, family Bible, rings, etc.
There are also two banners, one to the right and one to the left that are later joined to make one picture.)

Processional
(Bride and groom enter separately.)

RITE OF GATHERING

Call to Worship

Opening Hymn
(These are made inclusive and are printed in the bulletin when copyrights allow for this.)

Opening Prayer

Act of Reconciliation
(Passing of the Peace)

LITURGY OF THE WORD

Reading
Responsorial Psalm
(sung with choir or cantor)

Reading
(Response – soloist, etc.)

Reading

Communal Sermon
(All are invited to share words with the couple and
congregation as God's spirit leads.)

Pastoral Prayer

LITURGY OF CHRISTIAN MARRIAGE

Act of Visioning
(Couple shares a song or reading that demonstrates
their view of their covenant.)

Covenant with Families
    Pastor: This couple needs the support of their
families, for they cannot live out their vision alone.
Do you, their families, promise to continue to love
and to nurture them, to keep your lives forever
open to them that they, in turn, may love and nurture you?
    Families: We do.

Covenant with the Church
    Pastor: Do you likewise promise to love and to
nurture _____ and _____, to be open to their
friendship, to support them and to be supported
by them as they answer the calls of God in their
marriage and in their ministries?
    All: We do.

Covenant with the Couple

Pastor: _____ and _____, as you prepare
to enter into a new covenant with God, with one
another, and with the Church, we ask that you live
with faith in the coming reign of God, with hope
that you are called to its realization on earth, and
with love as if it were already here. Will you, in this
spirit, in freedom, and in truth now make your
vows.

Couple: We will.

Exchange of Vows

One partner then the other: I take you, as a gift
from God, to be my lifelong companion through
tears and laughter, sickness and health, work and
play. I will love you faithfully, constantly and
prayerfully, now and forever. Amen.

Exchange of Rings

One partner then the other: Take this ring as a
sign of my love and a reminder of our covenant in
God.

Unity Candle

(A song is shared during lighting of candle.)

Blessing of the Couple

LITURGY OF THE EUCHARIST

Consecration

Pastor: We ask all to extend a hand over the
bread and cup and to pray:

(In unison): Let Your Holy Spirit, O God, be
upon us and upon these gifts, that in our communion we may truly become one in the God and
Blood of our Savior, Jesus Christ, at whose invitation we now celebrate this Eucharist.

(All come forward and receive communion from
the couple.)

RITE OF DISMISSAL

Closing Hymn
(Some have used "We Shall Overcome" sung in a
circle.)

Dismissal

Postlude

SAMPLE TWO

Officiated by an Evangelical Lutheran (ELCA) minister, this marriage ceremony of Margaret Yackel and Mark Juleen took place at the home of the bride. The ceremony includes a song, composed and sung by the groom and a dance by the bride.

Prelude
Instrumentals for flute and cello
Solo: *Since You Asked*, by Dan Fogelberg

Processional
Jesus Shepherd
Our Song (The Circle of Love) composed and sung by Mark, dance by Margaret

THE MARRIAGE SERVICE

Scripture Reading
1 Corinthians 13

Homily
(by Pastor)

Hymn
The King of Love My Shepherd Is (everyone sing!)

Vows
> *Couple:* I promise to be faithful to you, open and honest with you.
> I will respect, trust, help, and care for you.
> I will share my life with you.
> I will forgive you as we have been forgiven.
> I will lead with you a simple, just, and peaceful life as Christ has called us to live,
> And with you I will work to further simplicity, justice, and peace in our world.
> I will love you and be thankful for the blessing of your love until death parts us.

Exchange of Rings

Solo
Ruby Jean and Billy Lee, by Seals and Crofts

Gifts of Flowers to Parents
The Gift of Love, by Hal Hopson

Hymn
For the Beauty of the Earth (everyone sing!)

Scripture Reading
Colossians 3:12–17

SAMPLE THREE

This is the wedding ceremony of Alice Ann Glenn, a Diaconal Minister in the United Methodist Church and Joseph Richard Turner, III, an artist. The ceremony took place at First St. John's United Methodist Church in San Francisco, California. It was designed to encourage the participation of everyone who attended. Music was also important to the couple and so is a key element.

Prelude
Vals Venezolano, by Antonio Lauro
"Gavott Chôro" from *Suite populaire brésilienne* by Heitor VillaLobos, Peter Shavitz, Guitarist
Variations on Greensleeves, Mary Ellen Novitsky-Hutchison, Flutist

Opening Words
Minister: Friends, we are gathered together here in the presence of God and with you as witnesses, as well as with the blessing of family and friends around the world, to join Alice Ann and Joseph Richard in holy marriage, a relationship which has been instituted by God. Norma will share with us how these two special people came to today.

(Mother-of-the-bride, shares a brief history of Alice Ann and Joseph Richard.)

Minister: Marriage signifies the mystical union which exists between Christ and the Church, the holy union Christ blessed with his presence in Cana of Galilee. Marriage is not to be entered into unadvisedly, but reverently, discreetly and in the awe of God. Alice Ann and Joseph Richard come to be joined in this union of marriage.

Scripture Reading
John 13:34

Statement About Marriage

(Minister and others take part.) Marriage is the most sacred of human institutions because no other ties are more tender, no other vows more significant. Its moral validity is dependent upon the free choice and honesty with which you enter into this relationship, or there is no true marriage.

Love, that strong and tender tie that will bind you together through all phases of your life, must be expressed through care and respect for each other's integrity, and so nurture the growth of each individual. As you live together, you will find that you are very human and that you will make mistakes, but one thing you must always remember is that your lives must rise above the petty things of life and find expression in tenderness, patience, loyalty, and trust.

A marriage brings two individuals into a unique relationship with each other – one which grows and develops as each continues to experience him or herself and others. Mature love is a union where each individual's integrity is preserved. Such love allows us to retain our identity as individuals. In love the paradox occurs that two people become one and yet remain two.

This celebration of marriage is an outward token of an inward union of hearts, which the church may bless and the state make legal, but which neither state nor church can create or annul, a union created by loving purposes and kept by abiding will. It is for us to acknowledge and witness the true marriage which already dwells in the hearts of Alice Ann and Joseph Richard. This marriage asks the blessings of God so these lives will be full of joy and the home being established will be one of peace and love.

Questions Regarding the Desire for Marriage

Minister: Joseph Richard, will you take Alice Ann to be your wife, to live together in marriage? Will you love her, comfort her, honor and respect her, in sickness and in health, and forsake all others and be faithful only to her as long as you both live?

Joseph Richard: I will.

Minister: Alice Ann, will you take Joseph Richard to be your husband, to live together in marriage? Will you love him, comfort him, honor and respect him, in sickness and in health, and forsake all others and be faithful only to him as long as you both live?

Alice Ann: I will.

Affirmation of this Union

(Unison prayer) O God, we ask that the promise and hope of this marriage be fulfilled. May the happiness and intimacy of this day be recalled many times. May this marriage be a source of independent strength and will; a reflection of connected lives; a recollection of the past; and a ribbon of love through the future. May Alice Ann's and Joseph Richard's anger at themselves and the world be honest and lively, may silence and despair never separate them, may they always return to each other. May we as friends welcome them again in other times and other seasons. In the years that lie ahead, may Alice Ann and Joseph Richard go from strength to strength. Should they fall, may we as members of their family, help them rise. Should we fall, may they help us, through the special gifts You have given them. All this we ask in Jesus' name. Amen.

Scripture
1 Corinthians 13 RSV (with music and dance)

Vows of Commitment

Minister: Alice Ann and Joseph Richard, what is your pledge to each other?

Couple (together): I promise, with God's help, lasting love. By love, I mean that I share with you my heart, my body, my soul, my mind and my strengths. Through good times and bad, in serious times and in play, I give you my friendship, loyalty, companionship, understanding, affection, trust, intimacy, honesty and respect.

These include: accepting you as you are and not as I think you ought to be, listening to you and understanding what I hear, discussing our differences, dealing with today's new challenges, forgiving each other, touching and silence when words fail.

I am excited to join with you, but not to dominate you. I pledge to cherish you in times apart as well as the times together. I promise to encourage your growth into full personhood as an individual and as my marriage partner. I know we can help each other learn and grow and I hope we can share learning and growth with others.

Readings

The Attitude of Love and *A Universal Love*, by Erich Fromm

Selections from *The Prophet*, by Kahlil Gibran

Blessing and Exchange of Rings

Minister: The wedding rings are the outward and visible signs of an inward and spiritual grace, signifying to all the uniting of Joseph Richard and Alice Ann in holy matrimony. Let us pray. Bless, O God, the giving of these rings, that they who wear them may abide in your peace and love, and continue in your favor, through Jesus Christ. Amen.

Joseph Richard: Alice Ann, I give you this ring as a symbol of my faith and love. I pray in Jesus' name for God's blessing on our marriage. Amen.

Alice Ann: Joseph Richard, I give you this ring as a symbol of my faith and love. I pray in Jesus' name for God's blessing on our marriage. Amen.

Statement of Marriage

Minister: For as much as Joseph Richard and Alice Ann have consented together in holy wedlock, and have witnessed the same before God and this company, and to this have pledged their faith to each other, and have declared the same by joining hands and by giving and receiving rings, I pronounce them husband and wife, in the name of the Father, and of the Son, and of the Holy Spirit. Those whom God has joined together, let no one put asunder. Amen.

Special Music

The Wedding Song, by Paul Stookey

Prayer of Presentation

Minister: Eternal God, creator and preserver of all humankind, giver of all spiritual grace, and everlasting life: Send your blessing upon Joseph Richard and Alice Ann whom we bless in your name; that they may perform and keep the vows and covenant they have made, and may forever remain in perfect love and peace, living according to your laws. Look with grace upon Joseph Richard and Alice Ann that they may love, honor, and cherish each other, and so live together in faithfulness and patience, in wisdom and true godliness that their home will be a haven of blessing and peace, through Jesus Christ. Amen.

The Lord's Prayer

The Kiss

Community Blessing

All: O God, we ask for Joseph Richard and Alice Ann the excitement of new discoveries and new creations, that their lives may be an adventure together, wherever they go. We recognize that love is not limited and cannot be contained. We ask that their love extend to their relationship with all people and to the world in which they live. Lord, make Joseph Richard and Alice Ann instruments of your peace. Where there is hatred, let them bring love. Where there is injury, pardon. Where there is doubt, faith. Where there is despair, hope. Where there is darkness, light. Where there is sadness, joy. Grant that they may not so much seek to be consoled as to console, to be understood as to understand, to be loved as to love. We dedicate ourselves to the continuing process of helping them to let their love so shine that it touches all who know them. Amen.

Recessional

Vals Criollo, by Antonio Lauro

SAMPLE FOUR

*This is the wedding ceremony of Kimberly Huff and
Stephen Bachmann. A Presbyterian (PC-USA) minister
who is a close friend of the couple presided. The sermon
includes personal words about the couple. The ceremony
also includes a time for witnesses to declare their love
and encouragement to the couple.*

Opening Words

Minister: Friends, we are gathered together this
day to join with Kimberly J. Huff and Stephen
Richard Bachmann in the celebration of their marriage. In marriage a man and a woman enter into a
spiritual and physical union, cherishing a mutual
esteem and love, bearing with each other's infirmi-
ties and weaknesses, comforting each other in trou-
ble, providing in honesty and industry for each other
and for their household, and living together the
length of their days as heirs of the grace of Cod.

Marriage, therefore, is not a state to be entered
into lightly or unadvisedly, but rather reverently,
discreetly, and with due contemplation of the deep
commitments and tender emotions which help
keep love alive.

For to be true, this brief and outward ceremony
must be but a symbol of this which for them is already inner and real – a sacred union of hearts
and lives which the church and state may sanction,
but which only God may bless, love can create, and
conscientious commitment sustain and fulfill.

Into this sacred relationship these two persons
come now to be joined.

Steve and Kim, such a union can be created
only by your loving purpose, be sustained by your
abiding will, and be renewed by your faith in one
another.

Declarations

Minister: And so now I ask you: Kim, will you take Steve to be your husband, to live together in constancy and devotion? Will you love him, comfort him, honor and keep him, and seek always to deepen the love you now profess?

Kim: I will.

Minister: Steve, will you take Kim to be your wife, to live together in constancy and devotion? Will you love her, comfort her, honor and keep her, and seek always to deepen the love you now profess?

Steve: I will.

Minister (to the witnesses): Will you who witness these promises do your best to offer love and encouragement to this marriage? If so, please say, "We will."

Witnesses: We will.

Reading

from *Letters on Love*, by Rainer Maria Rilke

Sermon

Ecclesiastes 3:1–11a.

Kim and Steve, with some trepidation and more trust, have given me permission to say a few words. When Kim and Steve announced their engagement at Thanksgiving, at least one person was heard to say "It's about time!"

It is time.

You have established your own identities and interests so that now you can enrich and complement each other.

To a large degree, you are not naive at this stage about relationships and the work they demand. Even the words you chose for this service indicate a keen awareness of the importance not only of love or commitment, but of ongoing trust in one another and in God's grace.

You've had time to begin growing together – to struggle with one another's strengths, weaknesses, and eccentricities; to share anxieties and frustrations; to discover talents you didn't know you had, like Steve's cooking and Kim's tennis.

So this is the time, this is the time to permanently join your gifts, your lives.

You have some fine gifts. Some of your gifts are ones you have in common – you're both crazy, wonderful, fun, crazy people who bring out the best of that in each other. You both have sharp minds and an ability to be critical, to say what you think, to be honest. And you both use those analytical skills and that forthrightness in your caring for others, because you both also have big hearts.

There are a number of ways in which you are different, too. And for the sake of brevity and sparing you some embarrassment, I will forego such things as who's the early riser and who's not, and mention instead, your pragmatism, Kim, and your creativity, Steve.

I see these as hallmarks of who you are as individuals and together as bellwethers for your marriage. I imagine that they are part of what attracts you to each other, what you give to each other, and I suspect that there are times or will be times when those traits make you feel your separateness from one another.

When I do weddings, I normally charge couples to tend their marriage as they have their courtship – to care for one another, to be open to change, to be ready to compromise, and yet also prepared to maintain your integrity as individuals. I think you know to do this, so instead I hope and pray for you that as you tend your marriage you will attend to the qualities, habits, and character traits that each one brings to this marriage as gifts – both those you have in common and those that mark you as different.

My other piece of advice is related – that is "to

speak the truth in love." I said earlier that one of
the gifts you share is an aptitude for honest communication. It's a gift that can serve you well. In
being open and honest with one another you care
for yourself, your partner, and your relationship.
In speaking directly to one another, your understanding of each other's needs and dreams can
grow. You will be able then to negotiate your differences and renew your excitement in one another.

But I want to underline that it is not simply honest communication, "speaking the truth," that is the
key, but "speaking the truth in Love." For the pledge
you make today is not just a profession of the love,
the passion, and caring you feel now, but a promise
to act in the spirit of love throughout the times and
seasons of your life, trusting one another in the ongoing process of establishing identities, working at
your relationship, celebrating your achievements,
grieving over losses, sharing your anxieties and joys,
cleaving to one another and becoming one flesh.

Charge

Minister: Steve and Kim, we who are gathered
here to witness your vows do so in the hope that
you will each live life more richly together. May
your hearts and minds and souls be knit ever more
closely together as you share the joys and perils of
life. We pray for courage for you when the way is
hard, and for humility when fortune favors you.
And when there is pain, may there be comfort, forgiveness, and peace. May your home help make
the world more homelike and may you find such
fulfillment there that you never cease to reach out
in love and concern for others.

Vows

Steve: I, Stephen, take you Kimberly to be my
wife, to have and to keep from this day forward,
for better, for worse, for richer, for poorer, in sick-

ness and in health, in joy and in sorrow, to love
and to cherish, till death shall part us.

Kim: I, Kimberly, take you Stephen, to be my
husband, to have and to keep from this day forward, for better, for worse, for richer, for poorer,
in sickness and in health, in joy and in sorrow, to
love and to cherish, till death shall part us.

Exchange of Rings

Minister: May I have the rings, please.

With these rings you declare yourselves wedded to each other. As you give, receive, and wear
these rings, remember the vows you have made;
for love is of God, and by the love with which these
rings are given and received shall they be blessed.

Steve: Kim, I give you this ring as a sign of my
promise.

Kim: Steve, I give you this ring as a sign of my
promise.

Pronouncement

Minister: Inasmuch as Kim and Steve have given
themselves to each other by solemn vows, with the
joining of hands and the giving and receiving of
rings, by the grace of God and the power vested in
me by the State of Michigan, I pronounce them
husband and wife.

Benediction

Minister: May these two people, now married,
fulfill this covenant which they have made, having
grown to trust themselves and each other, may they
be unafraid to accept the challenges before them.
Yet may they not only accept and give affection between themselves, but also nourish old friendships
and welcome new ones. We who love Steve and Kim
hope that the inspiration of this hour will not be forgotten. May they continue to love one another forever. Amen.

SAMPLE FIVE

*This marriage ceremony of Cindia Cameron and Steve
Rentch took place at a lodge at Lake Rabun, Georgia. It
was officiated by a Christian Church (DOC) minister, who
was also the mother of a friend of the couple. Included in
the ceremony is a reading given by two women from the
community where the couple's relationship began.*

Opening Music
(Wedding Party enters.)

Welcome
Steve and Cindia: I would like to welcome all
our friends and thank you for coming to share this
celebration with us. Some of you have traveled far,
and we are honored to have you here. You have all
been family to us and will be for years to come. We
have thought of this wedding as one of many gatherings we hope to have with you all as our lives
and families grow and change and intertwine.

Hymn
"Dona Nobis Pacem" (from *Rise Up Singing*, edited by Peter Blood-Patterson)

Blessing for Commitment
Officiant: Because Steve and Cindia have
purposed in their hearts to be joined in marriage
and become more completely one, this makes for
a holy occasion and something new is born in the
universe. I believe God brought you two together
and wills for you enduring love and happiness to
fill your cup of life to overflowing. Commitment is
to marriage what the heart is to the body. It is what
sustains life. Commitment is the core of love. If
you give yourself, Steve, unconditionally to Cindia,
and if you, Cindia, give yourself unconditionally

to Steve, this giving and this receiving will be blessed by God. It will mean you can conquer any differences, overcome any trials and difficulties. It means that your individual lives will be deeply enriched and the life you build together so ennobled that all who come to know you and those who are a part of your life will be blessed and will call you a joy and a blessing.

Reading

Barbara: Steve and Cindia's relationship spans the lives of many communities. Their relationship began in the context of a community in West Virginia, where Faith and I both live.

Faith: The community I shared with Steve and Cindia included countless breakfasts of sausage and biscuits before work with Cindia; and times like the night Steve ate supper with my children so I could attend a women's health conference; and the many evenings we ate together, talked politics, sang, and danced.

Barbara: Being part of a community involves not only memories of the past, it also means building together toward a future we believe in.

Faith: Community is sharing a vision of things to come and helping one another to come as close to that vision as possible right now on our jobs, in our circle of friends, in the intimacy of our homes.

Barbara: Marriage cannot be sustained without the love and support of the larger community. As Steve and Cindia commit themselves to a new relationship, we are called to recognize and to support them – as friends, as family, and as members all in the human community, connected to one another in a thousand mundane and mysterious ways.

Faith: We want to affirm the value of this marriage within the context of our community by saying, "we do."

Song

Since You Asked, by Judy Collins

Family Welcomes

Officiant: Because no marriage is only between two people but has a rippling effect, it involves the families from which these have come for a new family to be established. Will a member of the Rentch family welcome Cindia?... a member of the Cameron family welcome Steve? (Families offer words of welcome.)

Vows

Officiant: Cindia and Steve in their hearts have made their vows, but they have written them to share with us their commitment to each other.

Cindia: Steve, you have brought me this moment. You have given me your love, and the courage to open new doors in my own life. Your values of family, honesty, and humility and your ability to love and accept people without judging, have helped me to become more of the person I want to be. Therefore, I promise to share with you the brightest mornings of your life, when the sun washes the world with joy and beauty – I will be with you to share and remember. I will share the darkest nights of your life, those moments of sorrow and fear, when the world moves neither forwards nor backwards. I will share these moments and remember. And I will be with you on all those thousands of days in between, in the ordinary flow of life, to share the time and the threads which weave your life together. And your weave and mine will be one and we will grow and share and remember together.

Steve: Cindia, you have been a bright, warm ray of sunlight in my life. You have brought to me happiness and friendship; compassion and understanding. You have made me feel wanted and needed. Because of these and the many other things you have given to me, I stand before you and pledge my love and commitment to our relationship. I promise to be open and honest as best I can. I promise to respect you for the woman that you are and hope to be, to help you grow as you have helped me. I promise to stand by you during life's sad and troubled times as well as the happy and joyful ones. I promise to share my love and my life with you. I make this pledge to you in front of those people who mean the most to us both, our families and our friends. And I know that together we can make our lives as happy and fulfilling as we want. I pledge and promise to do that.

Exchange of Rings

Officiant: Now that you have pledged your love and commitment to one another by exchanging vows, would you have these vows sealed by a gift to each other? (Couple presents rings.)

O Lord, bless these rings that as they are given and received they may be recognized as an outward symbol of your eternal love and the love these two have pledged to one another.

(As the rings are placed.) These rings are of gold, precious: so let your love be the most precious earthly possession of your hearts.
These rings are made in a circle... without end... the symbol of eternity. So may your love be to all eternity. Now that Steve and Cindia have pledged their love to one another and have sealed that pledge with the gift of rings, I pronounce you husband and wife.

What God and your love have sealed, let no person tear apart.

Hymn

Officiant: Let us all join in singing *For the Beauty of the Earth.*

SAMPLE SIX

This is the wedding ceremony of Mark and Eileen Summit, the authors of Part 1, "Outward Signs of Inner Values." The ceremony took place in a Roman Catholic mission church in Santa Clara, California. The ceremony closely follows a Catholic Mass and includes a liturgical dance by the couple and two friends.

Processional Hymn
Trumpet Voluntare (Flag-bearers enter.)

Entrance of Families
(Mark and Eileen enter accompanied by their families.)

Welcome
(Mark and Eileen welcome guests.)

First Reading
Micah 6:6–8

Response
    All: To you, Yahweh, I lift up my soul, O My God.

Second Reading
1 Corinthians 12:31–13:13

Alleluia

Gospel
Luke 10:25–37

Homily

Exchange of Vows

Prayers of the Faithful

Preparation of the Gifts
(Friends prepare the table for communion.)

Eucharistic Prayer

Lord's Prayer

Sign of Peace

Lamb of God

Fraction Rite
1 Corinthians 12:4–28

Communion
(songs, *On Eagles' Wings*, and *Bread, Blessed and Broken*)

Meditation
"Here I Am, Lord" (with liturgical dance performed by the couple and two friends)

Recessional
(song, *Wedding March*)

SAMPLE SEVEN

*Written, in part, by Ellen H. Casey, a United Methodist
minister in Hope, Rhode Island, this service was originally developed in an attempt to resist excluding those of
Jewish faith or others, yet still remain a Christian wedding ceremony. It has evolved slightly from that form.*

*Two of the prayers (one which begins, "Spirit of Life"
and another which begins, "Source and spring of all
our joy and hope") are reprinted with permission of The
Pilgrim Press from* Flames of the Spirit, *edited by Ruth
C. Duck (Copyright © 1985).*

Introduction

Officiant: Family and friends, I welcome you to
this day of celebration. _____ and _____ have
invited us to share in their public declaration of
lifelong commitment to each other. You who gather
are an integral part of this ceremony. Your blessings, support, and encouragement are important
to this union, not only now, but in the days and
years to come.

Amidst the turmoil of our world, with all of life's
struggles and concerns, it is with deep joy and a
sense of wonder and awe that we pause to affirm
the power of love. As we gather to witness the union of _____ and _____ we celebrate the blessings we all cherish in our intimate relationships.
This ceremony calls us all to renew our vows of
love and commitment one to another.

Let us pray: Spirit of Life, your creative power
is seen in the whole universe; in myriad stars and
planets, and infinite space. And yet we dare to believe that you care for us and that you are mindful
of the things that we do. In your presence we gather
today, confirming a new constellation in human
relationships – the marriage [union] of _____ and
_____. Let your spirit be known among us, that

we may do what we do here with our whole hearts and wills, and that the commitment _____ and _____ make to each other may be a sign of your love on earth. Amen.

The Charge

Officiant: Through the wedding ritual, two persons declare publicly their intent to enter into a relationship of enduring love.

_____ and _____, it is absolutely essential that you realize the enormity of what you are about to undertake with these vows. Because you are human, and therefore, subject to error and temptation as all humans are, and because you have no idea of what the future holds for you... what joys and sorrows await you, your decision to marry [join] requires tremendous faith on your part.

You must have faith in yourselves as persons in your own right and in what you have to give to each other; faith in your relationship as a couple and in what you can do and be together; and most of all, faith in God and in God's presence with you to guide you in whatever the future holds. You must never forget that the marriage vows are not just vows of love, but they are vows of faithful love for each other grounded in God's love for both of you.

Declaration of Intention

Officiant: _____ will you take _____ to be your wife/partner? Will you show her your love by trusting her, treating her as an equal, and helping her to continue to grow? Will you affirm her and give yourself to her from this day forward?

_____ will you take _____ to be your husband/partner? Will you show him your love by trusting him, treating him as an equal, and helping him to continue to grow? Will you affirm him and give yourself to him from this day forward?

The Blessing

Officiant: Let us all remember that the path of love is meant to be walked together with all the human family.

All love is nurtured and guided by the love of others. Each of us counts on relatives, friends, and neighbors for the caring and concern that replenishes our own ability to love. _____ and _____ are joined together in a new way this day in the midst of the affection and friendship of you all and, most especially, in the presence of those whose love has been their life's companion, their families.

Who blesses this marriage? (Friends and families offer their blessings.)

Scripture

As part of this celebration, _____ and _____ have selected these scripture passages: (Selected readings are shared.)

Solo

Marriage Vows

Officiant: Let us pray. Eternal God, creator and preserver of all life, giver of all grace, Bless with your Holy Spirit _____ and _____. Grant that they may give their vows to each other in the strength of your steadfast love. Amen.

Partner: _____, I will share with you the joys and pains of life. I will walk with you when you are well, and will comfort you when you are sick.

I will honor you as a person.

I will respect your feelings.

I will let you know that you are special and that you are loved.

I will be your lover and your friend.

I pray that God will bless our marriage/union.

Other Partner: _____, I will share with you the joys and pains of life. I will walk with you when you are well, and will comfort you when you are sick.

I will honor you as a person.

I will respect your feelings.

I will let you know that you are special and that you are loved.

I will be your lover and your friend.

I pray that God will bless our marriage/union.

Exchange of Rings

Officiant: The wedding ring is an outward and visible sign of an inward and spiritual commitment.

Let us pray. Bless, O God, the giving of these rings, that as _____ and _____ wear them, they may be faithful to the love promised here and may abide in your peace and continue in your favor. Through Jesus Christ our Rock and Redeemer.

Partner: With this ring, I mark the promises I have made to you.

Other Partner: With this ring, I mark the promises I have made to you.

Declaration of Marriage

Officiant: _____ and _____, by your promises and actions here today, you have declared yourselves to be forever united in love. On behalf of all gathered here, I pray God's richest blessings on your marriage [union]. In the name of the Creator, Redeemer, and the Sustainer of Life. Amen.

You may kiss.

Candlelighting

Officiant: It was once spoken of a long married couple, "Those two shone like two flaming spirits bound into one fierce blazing torch." To symbolize their covenant of love, _____ and _____ will join the light of two candles into one.

Let us pray:

Source and spring of all our joy and hope,
by whose spirits our spirits are continually fed,
through whose mystery the meaning of our life
    is revealed,
by whose knowledge we come to know our-
    selves:
Be the abiding and unending presence with this
    man and this woman [couple],
when they know themselves to be deeply in love
and when they feel estranged,
when they experience elation,
when they know despair.
Because of your love that endures forever,
may their care toward the larger world be
    shaped by justice and tenderness.
May they discover that when they are faithful
    toward you and toward each other
their relationship deepens and grows.
Through the intensity of their life together
may they discover words that nurture,
gestures that heal, thoughts that illumine,
sharing those experiences
that turn life itself
into one continuing act of praise.

This we pray in the name of Jesus Christ our
redeemer who taught us all to pray saying, Our
Father...

Benediction

God gives love. God renews love. God is love.
Celebrate the love within you and let it overflow to
enliven all the world. Go now, and may the God of
love, joy, and peace be with you this day and always. Amen.

Recessional

SAMPLE EIGHT

This wedding ceremony of Georgia Lord and Lynn Leuszler was officiated by Georgia's brother, a Presbyterian Church (USA) minister. It includes readings by friends and family and contemporary music. It also incorporates a traditional Jewish wedding custom of drinking from a wine glass and then crushing the glass.

Opening Words

Ben (officiant): Friends, we are gathered here at this hour to witness and to celebrate the coming together of two separate lives. We have come to join this man, Lynn, and this woman, Georgia, in marriage; to be with them and rejoice with them in the making of this important commitment. The essence of this commitment is the taking of another person in his or her entirety, as lover, companion, and friend. It is, therefore, a decision which is not to be entered into lightly, but rather undertaken with great consideration, respect, and love – for both the other person and oneself.

The symbols of Lynn and Georgia's love for each other surround us. It is in the beauty of a sunset, in the freshness of a meadow in springtime. It is in the magic of the unicorns and in the promise of the rainbow. It is even in the tender beauty of the rose, which has traditionally symbolized romantic love.

Song

The Rose, by Amanda McBroom

Special Reading

Ben: Georgia and Lynn's friend Ed Senn will share with us a few words by Sir Hugh Walpole.

Ed: "The most wonderful of all things in life, I believe, is the discovery of another human being with whom one's relationship has a glowing depth, beauty, and joy as the years increase. This inner progressiveness of love between two human beings is a most marvelous thing; it cannot be found by looking for it or by passionately wishing for it. It is a sort of Divine accident."

Scripture Reading

Ben: To illustrate what they mean by love, Lynn and Georgia wish to read from 1 Corinthians 13.

Lynn: If I speak with the eloquence of men and of angels, but have no love, I become no more than blaring brass or crashing cymbal.

Georgia: If I have the gift of foretelling the future and hold in my mind all human knowledge and if I also have that absolute faith which can move mountains, but have no love, I amount to nothing.

Lynn: This love of which we speak is slow to lose patience – it looks for a way of being constructive. It is not possessive: it is neither anxious to impose nor does it cherish inflated ideas of its own importance.

Georgia: Love has good manners and does not pursue selfish advantage. It is not touchy. It does not keep account of evil or gloat over the wickedness of other people. On the contrary, it is glad when truth prevails.

Lynn: Love knows no limit to its endurance, no end to its trust, no dashing of its hope, it can outlast anything.

Georgia: It is, in fact, the one thing that still stands when all else has fallen.

Sharing Wine/Crushing Glass

Ben: Wine has long been associated with earth and life. The earth gives life to the grapes which turn with time and care into a rich wine. May you use life and time in a parallel manner to add new dimensions to your love. (Pours wine into glass;

hands glass to both Lynn and Georgia.) May you drink always from the full, and the empty will crush beneath you.

(Georgia drinks, then Lynn. Lynn wraps glass in cloth and crushes it.)

In accordance with ancient tradition, we wish that the years of your love be not less than the time it would take to fit these fragments together again.

Special Readings

Ben: Even intense love can be negative love. Love is negative when it traps or confines, or when it makes either of the parties to it weaker rather than stronger. Positive love yields strength and growth to those who share it. Ideally, the strengths of both partners can work together to compensate for the individual weaknesses of each. It enables both partners in a loving relationship to achieve more and be happier than either would on his or her own. Kahlil Gibran discusses this combination of loving support and individual strength in *The Prophet*.

Charlotte: (Reads from *The Prophet*, by Kahlil Gibran)

Ben: Antoine de Saint-Exupéry claimed that, "Love does not consist in gazing at each other, but in looking outward in the same direction." Lynn and Georgia share a desire for a world free from racism, sexism, violence, and injustice, a world enriched by a feeling of kinship and unity among all its people.

Song

Imagine, by John Lennon

Passing the Peace

Lynn: We hope you share this wish to live in peace and kinship with all people.

Georgia: We ask you to express this kinship now by turning to those around you and greeting them – with a hug, a smile, a handshake, or a kiss.

Encouragement of Friends

Ben: A partnership is a relationship of sharing. The partners in a marriage share its risks and benefits, its joys and sorrows. They receive its loving support but must be willing to work to make it succeed. Georgia and Lynn's friend Maybelle Ruppert will share a passage describing some of the challenges they must meet as partners.

Maybelle: On this day of your marriage, you stand somewhat apart from all other human beings. You stand within the charmed circle of your love; and this is as it should be. But love is not meant to be the possession of two people alone. Rather it should serve as a source of common energy, as a form in which you find the strength to live your lives with courage.

Today, as you join yourselves in marriage, there is a vast unknown future stretching out before you. The possibilities and potentials of your married life are great; and now falls upon your shoulders the task of choosing values and making real the moral dreams that other men and women have engendered and died for. In this way, you will create the meaning of your life. If your love is vital, it will make the choosing and acting easier for you.

As T.S. Eliot said, "We shall not cease from exploration, and the end of all our exploring will be to arrive where we started and know the place for the first time."

Declaration of Intention

Georgia: I wish to become Lynn's partner, to work with him to meet the challenges of our lives.

Lynn: I wish to become Georgia's partner, to work with her to meet the challenges of our lives.

Officiant's Comments

Ben: Lynn and Georgia, you have expressed your love for each other, the positive effect your love has on your personal development, and your desire to become partners in marriage. As you know, no minister, no priest, no rabbi, no public official can marry you. Only you can marry yourselves. By a mutual commitment to love each other, to work toward creating an atmosphere of care and consideration and respect, by a willingness to face the tensions and anxieties that underlie human life, you can make your wedded life come alive.

It is a long-established tradition that the officiant of a marriage has the privilege, if he chooses, of adding some personal comments relevant to the occasion and to the people who have come to make it a special one...

Blessings from Families

Ben: Georgia and Lynn have come today to be married. Do you, their parents, have any comments you wish to make on this occasion?

Edith: We should like at this time to speak of some of the things which many of us wish for you. First of all, we wish for you a love that makes both of you better people, that continues to give you joy and zest for living, that provides you with energy to face the responsibilities of life.

Melba: We wish for you a home – not a place of stone and wood – but an island of sanity and serenity in a frenzied world. We hope that this home is not just a place of private joy and retreat, but rather serves as a temple wherein the values of your life are generated and upheld. We hope that your home stands as a symbol of humans living together in love and peace, seeking truth and demanding social justice.

Ruth: We wish for you children – children who will not be mere reflections of yourselves, but who will learn from you your best traits and will go forth to re-create the values you have instilled in them. We hope that you will give your children the freedom to find their own way, that you will stand by them when they need you and will stand aside when it is time for them to seek their personal destinies. But we hope that you will pass on to your children the concept of family, not as an economic unit, but as a transcendent force which brings people close in time of joy and in time of need.

Ben: Will you, their parents, grant them your blessings and pledge them your love and acceptance?

Parents: We will.

Vows

Ben: Lynn, do you take Georgia to be your wife?

Lynn: Georgia, I take you as my wife. I promise to work to become the best person I can possibly be. I promise to help you become the best person you can possibly be. I promise that I will work with you, as an equal partner, to achieve what is best for us both. I promise to treat you always with love, tenderness, and respect. I love you. I wish to share my life with you.

Ben: Georgia, do you take Lynn to be your husband?

Georgia: Lynn, I take you as my husband. I promise to work to become the best person I can possibly be. I promise to help you become the best person you can possibly be. I promise that I will work with you, as an equal partner, to achieve what is best for us both. I promise to treat you always with love, tenderness, and respect. I love you. I wish to share my life with you.

Exchange of Rings

Ben: Lynn and Georgia wish to exchange these rings as symbols of their vows. In many ways this is fitting. The ring is an ancient symbol of everlasting union. The Greeks attributed such mystical qualities of perfection to the circle that when they discovered that this perfect form produced an irrational number in its dimensional relationship they concealed this fact. It is appropriate, however, that this symbol of marriage contains the imperfections of the man and the woman who create it.

Ben: (To Georgia) Georgia, as you place your ring on Lynn's finger, repeat from the Song of Solomon, Chapter 5, verse 16: "This is my beloved and this is my friend."

Georgia: This is my beloved and this is my friend.

Ben: (To Lynn) Lynn, as you place your ring on Georgia's finger, repeat, "This is my beloved and this is my friend."

Lynn: This is my beloved and this is my friend.

Declaration of Marriage

Ben: Lynn and Georgia, in expressing your private affirmations before this public company, you have pronounced yourselves husband and wife. You now face the prospect of a richer future than either of you alone could have looked forward to before. Because you have a richer future, you will also enjoy an infinitely greater present. From this moment on, go your separate ways together, remembering always to be each other's best friend. (Couple kisses.)

Lighting of Candles

Ben: The growth of love between a man and a woman enriches all humanity. It can add an increased tenderness and awareness to all those whose lives it touches. Georgia and Lynn wish to symbolize this touching with candlelight. Please light your candle from theirs.

This sharing of light indicates their wish that their love may add beauty to the world around them.

Song

Rainbow Connection, by Jim Henson

Planning an Alternative Wedding

Food, Flowers, and Festivities

Introduction

by Laurel Kearns

While my spouse and I were in the midst of planning our wedding, I never thought I would be able to say it was worth it. I only wanted it to be over. During that time, so many people told me they felt the same way about their own wedding celebrations. Unfortunately, they said they remembered very little about the whole event – "it was all a blur."

I am glad to say in retrospect I would not offer similar sentiments. Much to my surprise, our wedding turned out to be a truly transcendent and memorable event in our lives. In the midst of all the endless details, discussions, and lists, I had forgotten a wedding should be primarily a joyful, communal sharing of a couple's commitment to each other. It should focus on the couple's willingness to say to each other publicly they will join together to share in life's joys and sorrows. We were fortunate our wedding reminded us of what it was really about, but not without a lot of help from friends and the accumulated wisdom of my local Quaker meeting.

Along with other "experts" in the field, I'd like to share some of the ideas that worked and some things to think about that may help the whole process be less of an ordeal. We may overlook some crucial aspects with regard to your particular plans, but hopefully the bits and pieces we've selected to talk about will stimulate plenty of creative thinking on your part. We'll start with general thoughts, and then we'll look at specific issues related to the wedding ceremony and reception.

If you are considering an alternative wedding celebration, you have probably thought long and hard about your feelings toward traditional weddings. Knowing what you do not like and want, and why you don't, will help you immensely. However, don't underestimate the investment of others around you in that vision of a traditional wedding.

Cultural Pressures

As a culture, we are sold (and I use the word "sold" deliberately) a vision that is reinforced constantly. As you begin planning your wedding, you will find an incredible "wedding industry" that is invested in promoting weddings with lots of frills.

At every turn, you will encounter individuals who want you to buy fancy wedding clothing, and others who will encourage you to spend too much money on invitations, flowers, food, setting, and many other items. I was amazed at the constant pressure to spend money.

Don't let your wedding become analogous to Christmas, when the pressure to spend to make others "happy" often makes you miserable. You may have to work hard to find services that will accommodate your different vision, but remember, ultimately, you are the "buyer." You don't need to

One of our first decisions was that we did not want flowers. One of the women on the staff where I worked was known for her banner-making. We approached her with our growing concept of what our wedding would be and asked her if she would make a banner for us. The banner was beside the altar and a focal point for the ceremony.
    Alice Ann Glenn
    Monterey, California

buy into the vision of our consumer society. Better yet, you don't even have to buy at all, but can seek out alternative ways to celebrate.

In light of the incredible consumer pressure surrounding weddings, the best advice is to keep it simple. Set a budget early on in your planning and stick to it. If you happen to go over budget on one item, cut that amount from another item. Remember, rarely do the frills add to the most important aspect – the emotions and feeling of the event.

Pressures from Families, Friends, and Service Providers

You may not need the warning that often families and friends have an "investment" in that traditional wedding as well. While it is your wedding, it is also theirs in many respects. Families often see weddings as status events where they show others how much they "love" their child; or they repay friends and business associates, or they show the larger family and community what kind of an event they can put on. While this may all sound crass, you should be aware of the many undercurrents going on that can create family pressures for a certain kind of event. Family members often make up for their own weddings through those of their children or siblings, or they try to replicate nostalgic memories of their own wedding. Friends may be expecting to be part of the wedding party and will be disappointed if you opt not to have one.

Though it may lead to difficult conversations, talk to family members and close friends at length about their expectations, desires, and hopes; find out why certain things are important to them. You will benefit from knowing before the fact who is likely to have ruffled feathers and why. Some things may not be worth the price of offending a close friend

Harsh words, tension-filled moments, and decisions that were seen as selfish all stood in the way of our wedding being a grace-filled moment. In order not to make a mockery of the love we were about to celebrate, we decided to have a service of reconciliation. Family and wedding party were invited to the church for rehearsal. After the traditional practice, we invited everyone to take part in a short prayer time focusing on the theme of reconciliation. We prayed a common prayer asking for forgiveness and spoke a greeting of peace to each other. Finally, we joined hands and prayed together the Lord's prayer. This experience was a necessary and prayerful part of our marriage.

Nancy Parker Clancy
Troy, Michigan

We had heard horror stories about flowers for weddings costing thousands of dollars... What we did was both fun and practical. Before the wedding rehearsal and dinner, we loaded visiting friends and relatives into cars and went to the DeKalb Farmer's Market. Here each person chose a bundle of fresh flowers that attracted them... Back at the meeting house, we turned the kitchen into a florist's room (or nightmare). We had gathered many containers from home and friends, and we all worked together to make arrangements, corsages, and the wedding bouquet. I can't think of a better way for strangers to become acquainted than working collaboratively creating beauty. Not only did people who had never met before or hadn't seen one another for many years become friends, but we all enjoyed an entertaining afternoon.

Ann Bryn Houghton and
Vince Edward Brown
Atlanta, Georgia

or family member. At the same time, be clear that this is your wedding and you won't necessarily be following all of their wishes. If you get people's feelings out in the open early, you may avoid blow-ups closer to the event; you will also be able to make decisions with fuller knowledge.

Think through everything traditionally expected at wedding ceremonies and receptions – toasts, bouquets, the first dance, etc. Decide which aspects you want to incorporate into your wedding celebration and which ones you do not. Once you decide on wedding details, be clear with families and service providers what you plan to do. Often, the service people you hire will assume you are like everyone else, and they are there to help you have a wedding like everyone else. If you don't take time to think it all through, at the last moment someone will be expecting you to do something you hadn't planned on. In our case, we didn't want to cut the cake and feed it to each other, yet forgot to let others know. Thankfully, a friend's child appeared asking for the first piece of cake, and saved us from expectations we hadn't even thought to deal with.

At the same time, don't get so lost in details that you lose sight of the larger event. Few people will notice if everything is not perfect, nor will they ever know the things you forgot. Worrying over every detail will ruin the event for you.

Delegate Responsibilities

Most important, delegate responsibilities. Form a committee of friends, family, and community members who are most locally available to the wedding site. Let them take over planning, investigating, and carrying out tasks. The less you and your close family members worry about, the more all of you will be able to enjoy the event. Most people are more than willing to help because they don't want to see you so frantic and exhausted from planning that you don't enjoy your wedding day. Have the committee take charge of details on the day of the wedding, especially. You shouldn't plan to coordinate anything on the wedding day.

By delegating responsibilities, you should have time to take care of yourself. Get a massage the morning of the wedding, it will do wonders with all the accumulated tension. Take a quiet walk or a hot bath. Spend some time before the event quietly reflecting or meditating. Have breakfast with a couple of special people who will help you remain focused.

Finally, keep in mind weddings are joyful, collective events and much of that happens spontaneously. Don't make it into a performance or a carefully orchestrated party. At the same time, do plan enough to allow the joyfulness to come through.

After their wedding, a Thai couple chooses an older couple who has had a long and good marriage. The older couple goes to the bridal couple's marriage bed which has been made with fresh sheets and strewn with flowers. Lying on the bed, the couple dreams about their marriage and what they see in store for the bridal couple. The bridal couple then stands by the bed while the older couple tells them of their dreams and offers advice for a long-lasting, happy marriage.

Planning Pre-wedding Gatherings

by Heidi Roy

Historically, the engagement was the time when couples prepared for marriage (not just the wedding). Time was spent getting to know each other's families, gathering needed household goods, and being advised about marriage from others. Often, couples today spend their engagement time planning for an elaborate wedding ceremony and reception. They don't take time to discuss priorities, goals, and the shape they expect their lives to take. And too often, their pre-wedding parties focus on getting gifts rather than on celebrating with family and friends.

At a dinner held prior to a wedding ceremony, some Jewish couples and their families dine on bread and honey. The bread stands for the sustenance of life, and honey its sweetness.

Since our two families had never met, we held a family barbeque the evening before the wedding. This gave both families an opportunity to get to know each other before the actual wedding day.

Michael Schwartzentruber
and Margaret Kyle,
British Columbia, Canada

The informality of our wedding meant that we didn't need a rehearsal the evening before. Instead we had a softball game – the Shenk family and friends played the Schrock family and friends. The game was followed by cake and homemade ice-cream.

Carolyn Schrock-Shenk
Lancaster, Pennsylvania

At a pre-wedding party, a Dutch bride and groom sit on thrones under a canopy of evergreens. (The evergreens symbolize the couple's everlasting love.) Guests come up to offer their good wishes.

Gatherings and activities before the wedding day can encourage growth and can offer a sense of community support. Plan activities to foster family interaction. You might plan a simple party where close family, relatives, and friends of both partners share stories about the two of you and offer their best wishes.

Instead of having a traditional bridal shower, some couples are choosing to invite both men and women. And gifts don't have to be expensive, especially if you already have most everything you need. Guests can bring homemade gifts, for example, homemade preserves with recipe attached, or they might offer an invitation for a special meal at a later date. (See section on gifts for more ideas.)

Some couples choose a meaningful theme (i.e. a favorite book or season) and plan a party around it. Others incorporate family traditions or ethnic customs into special gatherings. Still others rethink the customary rehearsal and rehearsal dinner, opting for simpler celebrations including a picnic or hayride. One couple held a wine-tasting party to choose the wine for their reception.

Location/Setting

by Laurel Kearns

People celebrate weddings everywhere from a cathedral to a park, from a great hall to a barnyard. The money you spend on a location is not what makes your wedding special. Talk about what is important to you. Is it important to both of you that your marriage take place in a synagogue or church? Is there a place that holds special meaning to the two of you? What kind of setting would best serve the needs of your ceremony? If your church plays a large role in your lives, then your church might be appropriate. If you share a common interest in the outdoors, perhaps a local park or garden would be fitting. If your wedding reception will include a square dance, you might consider a park or, yes, even a barnyard.

Often the location of the ceremony is closely related to the location of the reception. You may want to use the same location, it may simplify matters. However, places often have restrictions on dancing, music, alcohol, hours, children, etc. Decide which of these are really important and make sure you ask a lot of questions. For instance, do they dictate your choice of food providers? If you decide not to go the usual catered route this could be a major issue. You should probably avoid locations connected with food, such as a restaurant or hotel banquet room, since they have such a large investment in your food choices.

Many people are attracted to outdoor wedding locations. If you are thinking of an outdoor setting, make sure you consider the many factors that are out of your control. Too much heat, humidity, wind,

We wanted to help my daughter make every aspect of her wedding significant. She began by choosing to have the wedding in the place where she had grown up rather than the place where she or the family was currently living. The date of the wedding coincided with local fiestas and Pueblo Indian dances. Following the wedding a supper party and dance were held at our little adobe house. After the festivities were over many of the guests camped out in the beautiful field by the river.

Virginia McConnell
Boulder, Colorado

Our wedding was very simple and celebrative. It was held in a local park with guest on blankets and lawn chairs.

Carolyn Schrock-Shenk
Lancaster, Pennsylvania

Our wedding was held outdoors in my parents' backyard where guests sat in a circle (symbolically surrounding us with their love and support) on hay bales which we rented for the day from a neighbor's farm.

Margaret Yackel-Juleen
Dundee, Minnesota

sun, rain, cold can make you and your guests uncomfortable or miserable. Don't expect the weather to be "normal" the day of your celebration. I have been to outdoor weddings in recordbreaking humidity in normally dry Southern California, and there were winter chills at a wedding I attended in late April. Our wedding day fell on the coldest day of the year – in mid-February after four weeks of typically mild southern winter weather. Furthermore, at many outdoor weddings, guests can't see or hear well. Also, bugs and noise can be terribly distracting.

Even though I speak discouragingly of outdoor weddings, many have worked well. Gatherings at state parks or area farms and inns, where people have the option to stay, and where multiple events can be planned – such as volleyball, hikes, picnics – often work well. If you really want an outdoor setting, check the place out thoroughly with the above considerations in mind. In addition, think about restroom facilities and seating, especially for older people.

Don't choose a location for its beauty alone. Consider the need to move indoors, or find an indoor setting with a nice view – large windows, a garden, etc. – and incorporate those views in some way.

Invitations

by Laurel Kearns

Bridal magazines, professional printers, and consumer pressures lead you to believe engraved invitations are a necessity. However, gold-embossed invitations, with tissue paper and numerous envelopes, can be both expensive and environmentally unsound.

Alternatives do exist. Consider making your own invitations. You can hand-write or type invitations, including relevant information. To add a more personal touch, include a poem or short essay that expresses your feelings about marriage. You might also consider drawing a picture or asking an artistic friend to create something for the invitation. You can have the invitations photocopied or "quick-printed" at a local print shop. Show your concern for the earth by using recycled paper, if possible.

If your wedding will include your church's congregation, you may be able to announce it in the church bulletin. If your wedding celebration will be small, you can offer invitations by word of mouth. One couple divided their guest list among family and friends who then extended personal invitations to others by phone. This approach fostered a friendlier wedding as the phone conversations paved the way for several new friendships.

Invitations usually deal with both the ceremony and the reception. Invitations are also the one chance you have to communicate a variety of related information. Be specific about details so people can plan accordingly. For instance, if you plan a long ceremony and/or a reception with dancing, let

Bob and I made the wedding invitations ourselves and had them reproduced by offset on stationery I got on sale.
Mary Margaret Velasquez Bertram
Palmyra, Michigan

Prior to our traditional Indian ceremony, my family bought and mailed invitations to family and friends who lived far away. Some relatives came for days early to help with the preparation and hand-delivered the rest of the invitations and gave oral invitations to these guests. Yatin's family brought and mailed invitations to his relatives and friends.
Alka Y. Patel
Jonesboro, Georgia

people know. Many people assume that a wedding celebration will be comprised of a 20-minute ceremony and an hour-long reception. You may also want to include information on lodging if you have arranged special rates for out-of-town guests. Consider including directions on how to get from the airport to the ceremony, and how to get from the ceremony to the reception, if relevant. If you plan a potluck reception dinner, you may want to suggest to local people the types of dishes to bring and where to bring them. (See the section on food, p. 104, for more on this topic.)

You may also wish to deal with the issue of gifts. For many of our local friends who knew us better than out-of-town relatives, we included a little card that suggested giving to an organization of their choice that represented both the giver and us, the couple. We enjoyed receiving notes explaining people's choices of organizations. Their choices revealed something about them and their perception of us. (See the section on gifts, p. 111, for more ideas.)

If you plan to invite children to the wedding ceremony and/or reception, consider offering childcare. Let guests know by including information in the invitation or on a separate card you slip into the appropriate envelopes. Make sure you ask people to notify you beforehand if they will be bringing children, how many, their ages, and to which events so you can make sure you have enough sitters.

Consider three other issues. First, you might want to indicate whether you will or will not change your name in any way to avoid any presumptions. Second, if you wish to include one or both sets of parents on the invitations, consider using parents' first names. By doing this, guests can become familiar with their names in advance. Finally, some form of R.S.V.P. is really essential in planning a reception.

You may find a variety of inserts for different people works best. I made up a number of inserts, not through a printer, but by using the italic mode on my computer and a laser printer. I then made copies of each insert on heavy ivory cardstock. You may also want to have an invitation "party" so friends can help coordinate it all.

INVITATION INSERT SAMPLE
Anne Sensenig and Daniel Erdman

1. Should we go through with the wedding?
     yes ____ no ____ maybe ____ later _____

2. If we do, can you come? yes ____ no _____
3. If you can, how many of you will there be?

____

4. If weather permits, would you be interested in volleyball? (Bring comfortable attire, just in case.) Croquet? yes ____ no ____

R.S.V.P. (*Respondez, s'il vous plait*) by May 16. Thanks.

We plan to have the wedding outside, so attire can be "semiformal." A light lunch will be provided.

I was reluctant to use the printed wedding invitation as the vehicle to head off crystal and china. Nonetheless, I realized I would be comfortable telling friends of my generation about our preference. Dividing up the guest list, Michael and I mentioned to our friends that we would like it very much if they would honor our marriage with a gift to the American Friends Service Committee, a Quaker service organization. My parents' friends were harder. I asked my aunts to meet me for lunch and I explained Michael's and my feelings. To my surprise, one aunt defended my proposal to the other by saying, "If nobody ever dares to do anything differently, then there can never be a change for the better." They decided they would write notes to the 40 or guests with whom they were acquainted just after the invitations went out. I asked that gifts in our honor be sent to the Highlander Center for community organizing and folklore preservation in Tennessee and gave them the address.
Bess Keller
Baltimore, Maryland

We asked guests to bring a garden flower to attach to our wedding canopy to symbolize their participation in a communal blessing on our union.

Margaret Yackel-Juleen
Dundee, Minnesota

The morning of the wedding, we went out to the (Vietnam) countryside on our Lambretta scooter and cut sprays of the most fragrant frangipani.

Earl Martin
Akron, Pennsylvania

In place of a flower bouquet, Native American brides sometimes honor their heritage by carrying brightly colored dried corn with husks attached.

Our friends made paper cranes and hung them as mobiles on each side of the stage.

Janie Howell
Ellenwood, Georgia

We asked people to bring a candle and holder (labeled with their name and phone number) from their home as symbolic of their roles in bringing light and warmth to our relationships.

Laurel Kearns
Atlanta, Georgia

Flowers and Decorations

by Heidi Roy

When deciding on decorations for the ceremony and reception, carefully consider the mood you want to create. If you choose to have flowers, think about collecting them from the gardens of friends and families, or pick wildflowers from a nearby field. You might also make arrangements from silk flowers that can then be used for other occasions or everyday. My sister recently used silk flowers to make table arrangements and bouquets for a friend's wedding. The couple sent many of the arrangements home with different relatives and friends. Couples can also donate flowers to a local hospital or nursing home. Like silk flowers, flowering or green potted plants also last long after the celebration is over.

In place of flowers, some couples create a festive atmosphere with colorful balloons and banners that hold special meaning. Still others prefer the simple, reverent mood of candles.

If you are planning an outdoor wedding, the natural beauty of the setting might be all you need. I was married on the third green of the golf course where my husband works. The area is surrounded by tall pines and is next to a small lake. The beauty of creation was all we needed to set the right mood.

Whatever you decide, just remember you don't have to spend a lot to create a celebratory atmosphere. Use your imagination!

Clothing

by Laurel Kearns

Couples spend much energy deciding what to wear to the wedding. There seem to be two lines of thinking. Most people believe that because a wedding is a special event, out-of-the-ordinary clothing is called for. As one friend explained her choice of a lacy gown, "it is your one moment to look special." It was important to her to look out-of-the-ordinary beautiful. A relative once explained to me that men wear suits all the time, therefore, tuxedos were called for.

Others believe the most important thing is not how you look but your commitment to each other, so it is important to feel like yourself in whatever you wear. When planning our wedding, I was determined not to wear an elaborate dress because it wasn't me.

Purchasing special wedding attire was not always popular. Until the mid-19th century, even the wealthy considered it an extravagance to buy a garment for only one day's use. If you choose not to spend a great deal of money on outfits that are worn only once, there are many alternatives. Some women choose to wear a handmade dress or to wear their mother's wedding dress. Men need not rent tuxedos, but can wear suits or even simpler attire. Others choose to make a personal statement about their lifestyle by wearing casual clothing that can be worn for other occasions. Still others prefer ethnic costumes to express their cultural background or that of other people they feel a special connection with.

When planning our vow renewal, our responsibilities as far as flowers and decor were minimal since the church would be brimming with wreaths and poinsettias. We ended up borrowing a single candelabra from my grandmother.

... On the gift table we had a small Christmas tree. The ornaments were family photographs from the past ten Christmases. In another corner, we had a bulletin board displaying photos, ads and news items of what was going on in the world at the time we got married.

Michelle DeLoach Harper
Forest Park, Georgia

I wore my mother's pale blue wedding dress, which had been modified so the lace from my mother-in-law's dress was inset over the sleeve material. There was also a detachable lace over-skirt made from my mother-in-law's dress. I wore the lace skirt over a plain colored skirt for a gathering we had after the honeymoon... I carried my mother's wedding Bible, inside which was her mother's wedding handkerchief.

Alice Ann Glenn
Monterey, California

Pat was stunning in her traditional Vietnamese ao dai wedding dress, a white floor-length skirt split to the waist with silky pantaloons. I borrowed a suit from Pat's brother who also worked as a volunteer in Vietnam.

Earl Martin
Akron, Pennsylvania

An Austrian bride often weaves myrtle, the flower of life, into her veil or headpiece.

Most importantly, when choosing wedding attire, remember that you are not going to a fashion show. Taking part in this special ceremony to acknowledge your partnership is more important than any clothes you wear. Make sure you are comfortable and you can move easily to perform the different parts of the ceremony.

The same is true for any attendants you might have. Dresses don't necessarily have to match, nor does men's clothing.

Rings

by Heidi Roy

Rings were originally thought to have been made of braided grass. Then later, they were fashioned from metal. The custom of giving a ring may have evolved from a time when a groom made a downpayment on the marriage agreement by giving land, livestock, or other valuables to the bride's family. When, in the 13th century, Pope Innocent III declared that a waiting period be observed between betrothal and marriage, it became customary to wear an engagement ring. The tradition of a diamond engagement ring began in 1477 when Maximilian of Austria gave a diamond to Mary of Burgundy to celebrate their impending wedding.

While in the past many people observed a single ring ceremony (one in which only the bride receives a ring), the double ring ceremony (where both partners receive a ring) is becoming quite popular. And the rings don't have to be made of gold and diamonds either. Some couples exchange family rings or have a jeweler design a wedding ring using a gemstone from another family heirloom. Others find beautiful rings in antique stores or have a local craftsperson design a one-of-a-kind ring that incorporates meaningful symbols.

You don't have to exchange rings at all, if you choose not to. Depending on your preference, you might choose another symbol that holds special meaning, say, a special locket or pendant; or you can use the money you save to support a worthwhile cause.

I gave my husband my grandfather's wedding band. He gave me his mother's 1920s engagement diamond. My wedding band is one my dad gave my mother.
Alice Ann Glenn
Monterey, California

In Ireland, *Clauddagh* rings are often exchanged. These traditional wedding bands are formed by two hands clasping a crowned heart and symbolize both love and friendship.

I did not want an engagement ring. (I don't care for jewelry.) This upset a lot of my friends and acquaintances, but gave me an opportunity to discuss the real meaning of betrothal.
Virginia Anton
Southbury, Connecticut

Food

by Julia Cade

When we conduct our marriage ceremony in the presence of others, we are creating a community of witnesses for this special occasion. You can extend the celebration and bind the wedding community by providing food after the ceremony.

Since food is something present with us everyday, the wedding planners may assume the matter of food will be very easy. This can be a big mistake because the food at a wedding celebration can be a production unto itself. For this reason, you should place special and concerted attention on the planning, preparation, and presentation of the wedding food – whether it is a simple meal or a feast.

Hiring a caterer is a standard way of addressing the food issue – but this route is costly and somewhat impersonal. You have several other options. You can ask a friend who is talented in food preparation to be the coordinator. This friend's labor and concentrated effort on planning and obtaining the food can be their wedding present to you. (The couple pays for the cost of food, but not for a caterer.) As a second option, you can ask a committee of friends (anywhere from six to a dozen) to plan, prepare, and contribute the food for the occasion. As yet another option, you can notify the guests that a potluck dinner follows and ask everyone to bring a dish. Other options may occur to you depending on what people resources are available.

Whatever option you choose, remember the food should add to the celebration, not detract from it. If you decide to ask a friend or friends to take care

Our reception was a picnic – sandwiches, fresh fruit, and sweet rolls that had been baked by friends.
Carolyn Schrock-Shenk
Lancaster, Pennsylvania

Instead of going through advertised caterers, ask around for smaller scale operations. By asking at a local natural food take-out and deli, I found a wonderful woman who was sensitive to my desires to have predominantly vegetarian food and to have lowered-sugar sweets. She was willing to cater appetizers, a few main dinner dishes, the cake, rental plates, etc., and to coordinate the serving of dishes brought by friends.
Laurel Kearns
Atlanta Georgia

My mother-in-law has a talent for food preparation and presentation. So her offer to put together a simple finger food reception was welcome. Without an extravagant sit-down dinner and headcount to worry with, we felt somewhat freer to expand our guest list.
Michelle DeLoach Harper
Forest Park, Georgia

of the food (or if you will coordinate the food), consider the time it will take to prepare and clean up. You don't have to follow the status quo and serve an elaborate, costly and timeconsuming meal. Simple, yet beautiful food can be quite meaningful and appropriate.

The food itself can be light fare as in a simple reception of finger food and beverages. Or, a talented friend can concoct and/or acquire a variety of dishes for a stand-up light meal. You can also have a simple sit-down dinner served buffet-style.

Several factors determine which is the best option to pursue. First, consider your budget. Even if you plan a potluck dinner or a committee of friends prepares the meal, there will be some costs involved for plates, utensils, glasses, beverages, tablecloths, etc. You can either borrow items needed or rent them. Consider using nondisposables in respect for the environment.

Choose a menu so both vegetarians and meat-eaters will be satisfied. The best menu, of course, is one where neither group even notices whether meat was or was not present. Some couples choose to include food that represents their ethnic backgrounds. Also, consider the social implications of food choices: Where did the food come from? Were pesticides used in its production? Is the food being boycotted for some reason?

Successful menus include foods people can prepare the day before (as opposed to on the spot). As you plan your menu, also consider the availability of refrigerators or stoves for chilling or heating any foods. Foods you can serve at room temperature or those which can be kept cool or warm easily are also more convenient.

Family members contributed food for the dinner – sort of a potluck with only family members making food. For example, my grandmother made all the tortillas by making them a few at a time and freezing them until the wedding day.

Mary Margaret Valesquez Bertram
Palmyra, Michigan

Since not everyone who attended the wedding came to our picnic reception, we had too much food. The caterer delivered the excess to a local soup kitchen.

Virginia Anton
Southbury, Connecticut

In Poland, a gift of salted bread and sweet wine is often presented to the couple. The meal symbolizes the bitter and sweet in life. Similarly, Lithuanian couples are served wine, salt, and bread. The wine symbolizes joy, the salt stands for tears, and the bread for work.

In Bermuda, the wedding cake is sometimes topped with a tiny cedar tree. After the wedding day, the couple plants the tree and watches it grow along with their love.

Traditional love-knot cookies are served at some Italian weddings.

In Jamaica, slices of wedding fruitcake are mailed to all friends and relatives that were unable to attend the reception.

The quantity of food you provide is also important. There should be a sense of celebration and lavishness as opposed to depletion and skimpiness. When planning food arrangements, make sure you neither over- nor under-buy. Try to figure how many people will attend the event. Some couples do this by requesting that guests return a response card. From your attendance number, you should figure everyone will have more than one of everything, including plates, forks, glasses, napkins, beverages, and food items. This can get tricky. Some people will have two helpings of something, while others will have four. Some might have only one or none, so figure on averages. I recommend you figure on 2.5 servings per person. In that way, you can accommodate both ends of the spectrum.

For a successful committee-prepared buffet for 50, six people can each make a festive salad of their choice that feeds 20 people (for a total of 120 servings, roughly 2.5 salad servings per person). You can then purchase two large smoked turkeys. Finally, six other people can each make a cake using the same recipe (for a total of 60 servings, 10 servings per cake).

You can plan a potluck menu somewhat by suggesting types of dishes according to the alphabetical placement of each guest's last name. For example, A-C, entrees; H-N, salads, O-Z, desserts. You might want to let guests know you have simple recipes on hand that are available at the guest's request.

Finally, take some time to think through food presentation. By using tablecloths, candles, flowers, baskets, and other items in presenting the food, you can really add to the atmosphere of celebration. Consider borrowing items from friends or purchase items which can be used again.

Entertainment

by Heidi Roy

In addition to food, entertainment is often a key element of a wedding reception. Many couples choose to have music, such as a pianist, harpist, a band, or a disc jockey. You can usually get names of amateur D.J.s or bands from your chamber of commerce, local colleges, and civic groups. You can also get names from other couples who have recently been married. When deciding on music, try to offer selections for all age groups. Also consider including some ethnic music and dances that are family traditions or customs of other people from around the world. One couple hired a square dance caller to lead the dancing at their simple, outdoor wedding.

Many forms of entertainment cost little or no money. Like some other couples, you might encourage guests to play volleyball, croquet, or go on a nature hike. You can also design a game that encourages friends and family to share stories and memories. Your options are unlimited.

The children presented a romantic play, "The Owl and the Pussycat" and had fun swinging at a homemade pinata.
Virginia McConnell
Boulder, Colorado

Our reception included several songs we helped to sing – It's So Bad for Me, by Cole Porter, and Will You Still Need Me (When I'm 64), by the Beatles. Also friends were invited to share poetry, stories or whatever.
Daniel Erdman and
Anne Sensenig
Lancaster, Pennsylvania

After a lively square dance, we held hands and formed a large circle, thankful for that day, for each other, and for everyone there.
Andre Gingerich Stoner
Lancaster, Pennsylvania

Photography

by David Pascale

We didn't want to waste our time posing when we could be visiting, so our brothers took some candid shots. Since they only took pictures of people they knew, we realize that we should have made a special effort to make sure we got pictures of everyone.
Virginia Anton
Southbury, Connecticut

At the guest book was a note asking our friends and family to step to an area where we had a video camera set up to record messages and memories that we will enjoy viewing in the years to come.
Michelle De Loach Harper
Forest Park, Georgia

When it comes to wedding pictures, you should strike a balance somewhere between the sacred and the profane. On the one hand your marriage, and especially the ceremony itself, is one of the most memorable and sacred events that will take place in your lifetime. When it comes time for two people to look at each other squarely and exchange vows which commit themselves to each other in relationship for a very long time, there is a particularly deep and powerful quality to the event. Even as a working observer looking for the right angle or anticipating the next shot, I have often been quite affected by the power of the ritual. From my experience, I don't believe you want to compromise this part. On the other hand, you probably do want some way of recording the event so that you can look back at it later and be reminded of what took place and of the people who came to share it with you.

Whether you use a professional photographer or not, I recommend you avoid two approaches. The first is the "tourist on vacation" syndrome. This happens when people are so busy posing for or taking pictures to look at later that they forget to be there in the first place. They relive what happened in a second-hand fashion. Your wedding will be more memorable not because of a carefully composed photograph, but from having experienced it as fully as possible, moment to moment. Let your focus be direct involvement in getting married rather than recording the event. You'll also have more fun.

Also avoid the "Hollywood extravaganza" syndrome. If you have a photographer, an assistant, as well as a video team, it tends to create a circus atmosphere. A friend of mine once photographed a wedding where the family employed some other people to do a video as well. She said you could hear one of the men from the back of the church giving directions over his intercom to the camerman up front. Even if done quietly, there is still the sense of a major studio production.

As far as wedding pictures are concerned, there are a number of ways to go with varying degrees of impact on the tone and character of your wedding (not to mention your pocketbook). Consider the following:

1. Find a friend to take pictures. You'll want to ask someone who considers herself/himself at least a serious amateur photographer, not just someone with a 35 mm camera. That friend must also be willing to give up a good part of his/her time to take pictures. It is a lot to ask of a friend since not only is s/he working, but it also cuts down on the time s/he has to socialize. This route often helps to keep things on a more simple and intimate level.

2. Ask a few designated friends to take snapshots. You can then collect the film and take it to the local drugstore for double prints, having enlargements made later.

3. Hire a professional. Most people go this route and it has distinct advantages: consistent quality, thorough coverage, experience, and the ease of just having someone else take care of it. Remember though, professional photographs don't come cheaply. Expect to pay anywhere from $400 to $7,500 depending on the album/package you select.

One couple made several disposable cameras available to guests. Guests were asked to take pictures during the reception, leaving the film for the couple to develop. (With concern for the environment and its resources, you may instead ask that people bring cameras from home.)

I recently attended a marriage ceremony for a French groom and U.S.A. bride. It was a wonderful blend of French and U.S.A. custom. One of the French traditions impressed me. Immediately following the ceremony, everyone assembled outside the church for a group picture with bride, groom, parents, attendants, and families.

Deanna L. Shimko-Herman
Waterford, Wisconsin

To find a professional you will be happy with, ask for recommendations from people you know who have had weddings and take a look at their pictures. Question them particularly about the attitude and approach of the photographer, about how well the photographer listened to what they wanted and respected their wishes.

4. Another option is to hire a professional to shoot the wedding in the style you prefer and then have him/her give you the film at the end of the day. The pro gets a flat fee of $200 to $400 plus film costs. You get the film developed and have prints made as you see fit. Most pros do not like to do this since they make more money selling you albums and prints.

That brings us to the question: What do you really want to end up with? There is such a variety of albums and packages available in all kinds of sizes and with all kinds of add-ons and extras. Couples often get caught up in the spending frenzy associated with weddings and order some costly and unnecessary things. Take time to think about it beforehand when heads are cool.

Do you want a big album at all? Along with your shirts and socks, they usually end up in closets and drawers. Maybe an album of 4 x 5s would be better with a couple of larger prints to hang on the wall. Or instead of a fancy album, you might want to put your own together, a more down-home version. Also consider whether or not parents need albums as well, or if a few select photos would serve just fine.

Just remember that the choice is yours. Wedding photography is a business and professionals will try to sell you. Ask yourself, "Ten years down the road what will we need, in terms of photography, to remember our wedding day?"

Gifts

by Alexander Jacobs

"Let us pray for all the families throughout the world.

"Gracious God, you bless the family and re-new your people. Enrich husbands and wives, parents and children more and more with your grace, that strengthening and supporting each other, they may serve those in need and be a sign of the fulfillment of your perfect kingdom, where, with your Son Jesus Christ and the Holy Spirit, you live and reign, one God through all the ages of ages. Amen."

Lutheran Book of Worship, p. 204

The above prayer is all too frequently *not* requested by a marrying couple. Its focus is clearly not on the couple, but on the larger world into which the two are now launching out as wife and husband. The prayer presumes that a wedding celebration is representative of our understanding of steward-ship and justice (Amos 5:21–24), as are all of our church celebrations. The prayer describes marriage and family life as a "sign" to others and the world of what the kingdom of God will be like.

It is significant that Jesus' first "sign" was per-formed at a wedding at Cana in Galilee (John 2:7–11). Jesus provided the celebrants not with what they wanted, but with what they needed. The "sign" not only met needs, it engendered faith and wor-ship. Our own celebrations and gift-giving will, whether we intend them or not, express our un-derstanding of justice and stewardship.

Recently one of our neighbors offered to donate five electric frying pans to our loan closet for interna-

When women in my home church of Aztec, New Mexico said they wanted to give me a shower, I was apprehen-sive... imagining all sorts of electric frying pans, electric can openers, electric blankets, etc. So I wrote... expressing my concern about exploita-tion of natural resources and [saying] I would prefer it if items which were used but still good could be given as gifts – as a form of recycling. I also included a list of items we needed, such as wooden clothesdrying racks, garden tools, trash cans. We didn't receive anything that was use-less or wasteful, but we did receive practically everything on the list. The most wonderful part was that nearly every-thing was stuff people had had tucked away in closets for years and no longer used, or the gifts were handmade by the women.

Anne Doerfert McGoey
Taos, New Mexico

We sent out a wedding announcement that read: "Your presence with us is the greatest gift you can give us. WE REQUEST NO GIFTS. We have combined two well-established homes and we have need of nothing. If you feel you would like to share with us, please make a donation to a people-serving organization and tell us about it." And we suggested some groups they might give to. Many folks gave money to places we suggested, including a scholarship fund in my dad's name... And as we celebrated our 12th wedding anniversary, we got good news from my alma mater that enough money had accrued in the scholarship fund that the first one would be given this year!

Alice Ann Glenn
Monterey, California

Instead of gifts, we asked our guests to bring a favorite dish to share at our potluck reception. And we asked them to bring some time. Our mothers told stories of our earlier years; we played games and sang more songs. Friends made a calendar and for each month someone committed themselves to send us a favorite tape or book, to take us out to

tional students. I was grateful, but had to ask, "why five?" Her answer: "Because that's how many I have. Actually I did have seven; I'm keeping one and I gave one away." She and her husband have been married for ten years and these frying pans were wedding gifts they had been storing in their attic.

Each year, people in North America spend well over $200 million on wedding gifts. We need to rethink the way we go about giving gifts! It used to be that when a couple got married, gifts were essential to their life together as a family and were visible support from the community that surrounded them. In many places and circumstances, this is still the case. If the couple really needs material items, it is appropriate to give gifts that respect others and the earth. Consider gifts that are both useful and beautiful. Give gifts made by local or Third-World craftspeople, or make a gift yourself.

On the other hand, because of the relative affluence of many in our society there is often no real need to shower the bride and groom with frying pans and toasters. There are an increasing number of first and second marriages where the couple is already established. When I was married for the second time, my wife and I had all we needed between the two of us to set up house and live comfortably.

In this situation, we can be both good stewards and appropriate gift-givers at the same time. When the son of a very wealthy friend was married in Los Angeles, we gave a gift to the Sanctuary Movement. When my soon-to-be-M.D. niece was married we gave a gift to Children's Hospital. And we gave a gift to Habitat for Humanity for my realtor cousin's wedding. Most everyone who has received a gift to a worthy cause in their honor has been both pleased and gratified.

The initiative for alternative gift-giving lies not only with the giver. When planning their wedding, a couple can express their faith by suggesting useful gifts they need or recipients of gifts of money or other items, and can include this with the invitation. When counseling for marriage, clergy should include appropriate gift-giving as a portion of the planning. We can no longer just go along with the consumerism of our culture as if there are no alternatives.

Criteria for wedding gifts go far beyond "etiquette." They signify whether the pattern of our life together will be one of "getting" or one of "sharing." A wedding is a perfect moment to express our interconnection with the larger web of life and love that we call Creation.

eat, or some other treat. Folks wrote messages which we took along and read on our honeymoon at the shore.

Andre Gingerlich Stoner
Lancaster, Pennsylvania

We chose to keep the objects that were given to us, but to give away the money.

Kathie Klein
Atlanta, Georgia

As table decorations we bought several variegated plants which doubled as gifts for members of the wedding party.

Paula Meador Testerman
Wake Forest, North Carolina

In Italy, the groom often gives the bride a doll as a wedding keepsake.

We asked friends to save rose petals from their rose bushes. We then threw the dried petals instead of rice or confetti.

Mike Schwartzentruber
and Margaret Kyle
British Columbia, Canada

At the home of an older friend, I recently saw a beautiful friendship quilt. When she became engaged, each female relative embroidered one white muslin square with her own name in the middle along with birds, flowers, or any design she chose. An elderly aunt who was blind wrote her name in pencil and her daughter embroidered it for her. The squares were assembled into a quilt top and quilted by her mother and sisters. It made a beautiful, lasting, practical, and inexpensive gift, although it took some effort. Each member of her family had one as it was always their gift to each other.

Sheryl Craig
Warrensburg, Missouri

Other

There are a number of other issues you may want to discuss. The following is a partial list:

- who is paying for the wedding
- seating arrangements
- childcare
- toasts
- cutting the cake
- a receiving line
- throwing the bouquet and garter
- special dances (wedding party dance, father/daughter dance, dollar dance, etc.)
- guest book
- thank-you notes
- honeymoon

Finally, remember no matter how much you plan, no wedding is flawless. Even if the flowers wilt and the food gets cold, your wedding will be "perfect" because it celebrates the special union of two people.

Contributors

Laurel Kearns, Ph.D., serves as Assistant Professor of Sociology of Religion at Drew Theological School, Madison, New Jersey. Much of the information she shares came out of planning her own wedding.

Julia Cade is a writer, legal consultant and freelance caterer in Washington, DC.

David Pascale is a professional photographer living in Atlanta.

Alexander Jacobs is an ELCA (Evangelical Lutheran Church in America) campus pastor with the Metro Milwaukee Campus Ministry.

Heidi Roy is the editor for Alternatives Lifestyles Inc.

Some people don't think children belong at weddings; for us, it was more important that the wedding was a truly collective, communal, inclusive event. Particularly at the reception, we received many thanks for providing sitters so that the children could be a part of the fun and yet the parents could enjoy the event also.

Laurel Kearns
Atlanta, Georgia

Instead of a guest book, we had a poster. It contains an Apache Wedding Blessing that we had done in calligraphy. All the guests signed under it. It hangs in our living room.

Alice Ann Glenn
Monterey, California

Wedding Timeline/ Checklist

The following checklist will help you plan your wedding celebration. Remember, however, that these are only suggested guidelines. While this timeline proposes beginning your planning as much as four to six months ahead of time, many beautiful weddings have been planned in less time.

Read through the guidelines and check "To Do" next to those that are relevant to your celebration. Later, check the "Done" column when the items are completed.

As Soon as Possible

To Do	Done	
_____	_____	Decide on type of wedding and reception you will have.
_____	_____	Develop a wedding budget. Talk about how expenses will be paid.
_____	_____	Choose an officiant and location. Meet with the officiant to discuss ceremony requirements and pre-wedding counseling needs.
_____	_____	Set a wedding date and reserve wedding locations (church and reception.)
_____	_____	Meet with ceremony musicians. Ask for guidelines and suggestions.
_____	_____	Begin to create your own ceremony. Talk with your partner and families about various aspects and traditions.

To Do	Done	
_____	_____	Choose music for the ceremony (opening music, processional, recessional, songs, and hymns.)
_____	_____	Discuss and choose scripture readings and other special readings.
_____	_____	Begin to write your vows, etc.
_____	_____	Plan ceremony format and discuss with officiant.
_____	_____	Choose attendants if you wish to have any.
_____	_____	Choose wedding attire.
_____	_____	Choose rings or other symbols.
_____	_____	Begin making a guest list.
_____	_____	Plan reception entertainment. Choose musicians, if needed.
_____	_____	Decide on decorations. Visit florists or others who will help with decorations.
_____	_____	Choose food coordinator(s) and discuss menu options.
_____	_____	Choose a photographer, if needed.
_____	_____	Plan pre-wedding gatherings. Introduce your families if they do not already know one another.

Three Months Before

To Do	Done	
_____	_____	Talk about what kinds of gifts might be appropriate. Do you want to make gift suggestions to guests? How?

To Do	Done	
_____	_____	Register at a store and/or choose a social justice organization(s) to receive gifts.
_____	_____	Design invitations.
_____	_____	Order flowers, banners, balloons, etc.
_____	_____	Finalize guest list.
_____	_____	Participate in pre-wedding counseling.
_____	_____	Visit doctor for complete medical examinations, including blood tests.

Two Months Before

To Do	Done	
_____	_____	Address and mail invitations.
_____	_____	Confirm dates and arrangements with officiant, food coordinator(s), musicians, etc.
_____	_____	Meet with officiant about final ceremony plans and contents. Make sure that any requirements are included.
_____	_____	Make arrangements for rehearsal and dinner, if needed.
_____	_____	Plan lodging and transportation for out of town guests.
_____	_____	Decide on honeymoon plans and make reservations, if needed.
_____	_____	Decide where you will live after the wedding.

One Month Before

To Do   Done

_____   _____   Apply for marriage license.

_____   _____   If you plan to change your name(s), do so on credit cards, drivers' licenses, social security cards, bank accounts, etc.

_____   _____   Make sure wedding attire fits properly.

_____   _____   Get any accessories needed for attire.

_____   _____   Choose gifts for attendants and partner, if desired.

Two Weeks Before

To Do   Done

_____   _____   Check with officiant about final ceremony details.

_____   _____   Choose or borrow unity candles, if needed.

_____   _____   Send notes to ceremony participant about rehearsal time and date. Include dinner invitation, if needed.

_____   _____   Design and prepare wedding bulletins, if needed.

_____   _____   Count R.S.V.P.s and give food coordinator a final number.

_____   _____   Make seating charts if you are planning a sit-down dinner.

_____   _____   Send wedding announcement to newspapers, if desired.

_____   _____   Send thank-you notes for all gifts received so far.

One Week Before

To Do	Done	
_____	_____	Have a final consultation with the officiant and wedding service providers or friends, including those who will be providing music, decorations, food, photographs.
_____	_____	Begin packing for honeymoon, if necessary.

The Day Before

To Do	Done	
_____	_____	Wash and clean cars.
_____	_____	Attend the rehearsal, if needed.
_____	_____	Place fees/gifts for officiant, musicians, and others in sealed envelopes and choose a person to distribute them on the wedding day.
_____	_____	Pack an emergency bag – tissues, aspirin, needle, thread, safety pins, pantyhose, etc.
_____	_____	Relax!

Budget Worksheet

Before you begin to talk about wedding expenses, spend some time discussing who will pay for the wedding. If people other than the two of you will pay for your wedding, involve those people as you talk about and set a budget. This budget sheet will help you keep track of your decisions and actual costs. If you spend more on one item than your budget allows, balance it out by taking that amount from another item. *Remember, just because an item is listed here doesn't mean it has to be part of your celebration.*

	Budget	Actual
Pre-Wedding Gatherings		
Engagement party	_____	_____
Wedding shower	_____	_____
Rehearsal dinner	_____	_____
Other	_____	_____
Other	_____	_____
Location Fees		
Ceremony	_____	_____
Reception	_____	_____
Other	_____	_____
Other	_____	_____
Stationery		
Invitations	_____	_____
Inserts (R.S.V.P., etc.)	_____	_____
Thank-you notes	_____	_____
Wedding bulletins	_____	_____
Postage	_____	_____
Other	_____	_____
Other	_____	_____

	Budget	Actual

Decorations

	Budget	Actual
Flowers	_____	_____
Banners	_____	_____
Balloons	_____	_____
Candles	_____	_____
Other	_____	_____
Other	_____	_____

Clothing

	Budget	Actual
Bride's attire	_____	_____
Groom's attire	_____	_____
Accessories	_____	_____
Attendants' apparel	_____	_____
Other	_____	_____
Other	_____	_____

Rings/Symbols

	Budget	Actual
Bride's	_____	_____
Groom's	_____	_____
Other	_____	_____
Other	_____	_____

Food

	Budget	Actual
Food coordinator	_____	_____
Servers	_____	_____
Food	_____	_____
Wedding cake	_____	_____
Beverages	_____	_____
Gratuities and taxes	_____	_____
Utensils	_____	_____
Chairs	_____	_____
Tables	_____	_____
Tablecloths	_____	_____
Decorations/presentation		
Other	_____	_____

	Budget	Actual

Entertainment

	Budget	Actual
Wedding musicians	_____	_____
Reception musicians	_____	_____
Disc jockey	_____	_____
Square dance caller	_____	_____
Sports equipment rental	_____	_____
Other	_____	_____
Other	_____	_____

Photography

	Budget	Actual
Wedding album	_____	_____
Parents' albums	_____	_____
Video recording	_____	_____
Other	_____	_____
Other	_____	_____

Gifts and Fees

	Budget	Actual
Officiant	_____	_____
Custodians	_____	_____
Transportation	_____	_____
Guest accommodations	_____	_____
Honeymoon	_____	_____
Other	_____	_____
Other	_____	_____

TOTAL

_____   _____